Falling into Place

*John Terpstra* (signature)

# Falling into Place

## John Terpstra

ILLUSTRATIONS BY WESLEY BATES
MAPS BY GLENN MACDONALD

GASPEREAU PRESS  PRINTERS & PUBLISHERS  MMII

THE LAY OF THE LAND

Introduction 11

The Big Picture 15

*Lay-by* 21

So pleased with this place 25

*Lay-by* 39

The whole night going on without us 41

*Giants* 45

*Lay-by* 49

Motion and Memory 51

*Lay-by* 69

Oriah Mountain Dreamer 71

*Ceremony* 81

Head of the Lake 83

Selective Memory 109

Selective Memory: *Always Fresh* 115

Mercer's Glen 117

The stuff we're made of 143

Mr. McQuestion 151

*Blondin on a Tightrope* 163

Where Here Is 167

The Jump   179

The whole night going on without us   185

*Lay-by*   201

Looking for the Sandbar   205

Submission to an Unannounced Competition   221

Brother Nick and the Centre of the Earth   225

Selective Memory: The Doll's Leg   229

A Gruesome Ground   237

Falling into Place   247

A Slow Undressing   253

Flight and Refuge   263

*Lay-by: lectio divina*   279

*St. Terra*   283

Selective Memory: "*I want to live here...*"   285

MacNab's Favour   293

Two Hundred Years to the Day   305


Selected Bibliography   315

Acknowledgements   317

MAPS  The Niagara Peninsula  13

Head of the Lake  47

Burlington Heights  65

Mercer's Glen  113

ILLUSTRATIONS  Parked at the Lay-by  22

Cootes Paradise from the
High Level Bridge  34–35

Hamilton Harbour (Burlington Bay)
from the High Level Bridge, with
Carroll's Point in the foreground  36–37

End of the Iroquois Bar  85

Mercer's Glen  138

Iroquois Bar, from Carroll's Point  181

The cholera stone  238

Iroquois Bar, from Cootes Paradise  281

# Falling into Place

# Introduction

THIS BOOK is what happens when one person becomes completely enamoured of the landscape, and a particular feature of the landscape, in the city where he lives.

NIAGARA PENINSULA  *detail on page 47*

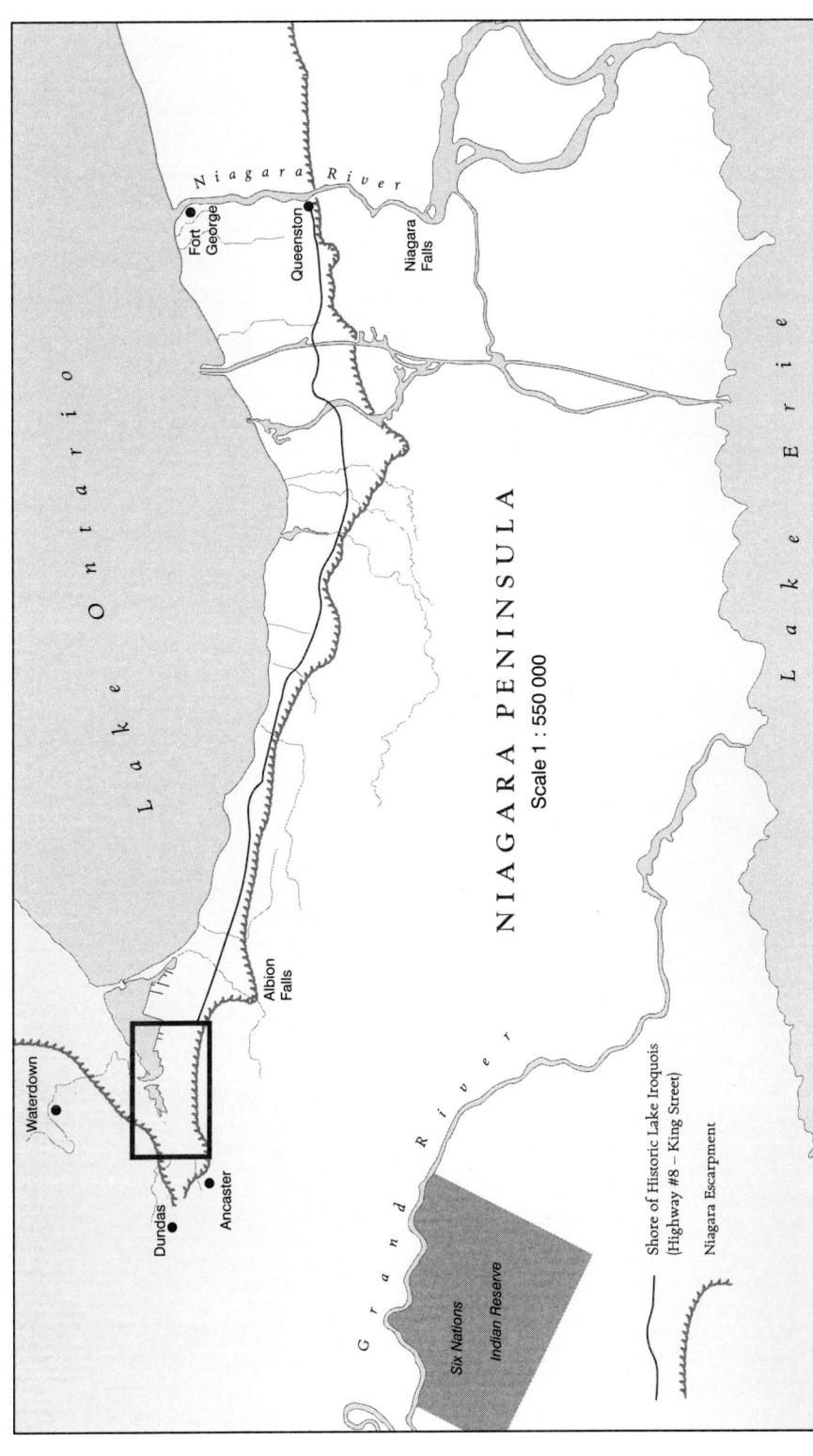

# The Big Picture

I AM ATTACHED TO A PIECE OF GEOGRAPHY ...
The words rolled off the top of my tongue and into the closed air of the car as unexpectedly as if a single wave had broken onto a beach and laid twelve small pebbles, one for each syllable, in sequence on the sand.

I was driving along a stretch of the road that takes me to work. It's the only road that will take me there, unless I want to circle the bay that lies to my right and add thirty kilometres to a ten-minute drive. Or I could go around the smaller body of water that lies to my left, which would add only ten kilometres. I sail instead between these two bodies, on a road that rides one hundred feet above their surface level, on the crest of a long and narrow piece of geography to which I have just declared attachment.

The water recedes from around the words as I turn off the road, and down. Twelve round pebbles, lying in the sand.

THE ELONGATED LANDFORM in question is a sandbar. An old, retired sandbar. A part of the body of earth no longer doing or being what it once did or was. A relic. Half the bar lies beached like a whale on the shore of the bay, a landlocked swell under the streets and houses of the city. The other half is water bound, stretching out across the bay, looking peninsular, looking like nothing so much as one of those features of the Dutch landscape, a dike.

A sand-*and-gravel* bar, to be more precise. And geographer's gravel, not crushed-stone: one size up from a grain of sand, and rounded. There's also pebble and cobble in the bar, which are the two sizes up from gravel. Like many of us who live around, beside and atop this feature of the landscape, the stuff the bar is made of comes from elsewhere. Pushed and dragged all the way, the sand, gravel, pebble and cobble were deposited here by ice-age glaciers as unceremoniously as immigrant ships discharging their cargoes of humanity. As the ice began to retreat, a tongue of running water carried the stones the last little way to their new home. This new home was at the place where the meltwater stream met the waves of a lake filled with melted ice. Our current lake, Ontario, only half-fills the bowl of its predecessor, and is a comparative pond. The sandbar was part of the former lake's shoreline when much of where we live, we who live here now, was under water.

I AM ATTACHED TO a superannuated earthwork. A geographical speed bump.

Three stoplights into the city, you may find yourself waiting on the top of a small rise that raises the body temperature of walkers and cyclists but barely depresses the foot on the accelerator. On green, five lanes of traffic descend into downtown, wading along the bed of Lake Iroquois. City Hall is submerged to its third floor: Planning Department. There are no plans in place for the possible return of a glacial lake, though it might be prudent. The waters, frozen and freed, have come and gone more than once.

My drive to work begins on the meltwater side of the sand-and-gravel bar. But this is a small city. Within a few minutes of leaving home, I am ascending a street that ends at a set of traffic lights that stands on the bar's spine. Where I wait for green is also where the sandbar leaves the city proper, and sets out across the bay.

In physiography circles, this six-kilometre-long physiographic feature has a name: the Iroquois Bar. The half of the Bar that stretches out across the water also has a common, equally unfamiliar name.

In 1793, having just returned from travelling the length of the province making preparations for an event he thought inevitable—an invasion from the south by the Americans—Lieutenant-Governor John Graves Simcoe wrote *Burlington Heights* across this piece of geography that reminded him of a place back home, in England. He was at his home-away-from-home, Kingston, farther up the lake, making maps of the landscape of his travels, of places with few settlements, fewer roads, and a lot of geography. He was attaching tags to landmarks and features for strategic reasons, and at the same time giving the people who had begun to live in those places names for their new home.

During his travels Simcoe had paid a visit to Richard and Henrietta Beasley. The couple were among the area's first white settlers. They lived in a log cabin on the shoreline of the bay, at the base of the Iroquois Bar, below where a large, elegant old house now stands, facing the idler waiting for the light to turn green. The house is called Dundurn Castle.

Dundurn stands a little lower than the road, and the idler can gaze into its second-storey bedroom windows while waiting. From the other side of the bedroom the view looks over the bay, and down into the ravine where the Beasleys' cabin stood.

Left on green. Cruising York Boulevard, along the crest of the Iroquois Bar, Burlington Heights subdivision. The name hasn't stuck through the two centuries, and a person hearing it today is more likely to think it refers to a housing development in the nearby city of Burlington, farther up the bay, than to this piece of geography.

A cemetery scrolls by on the driver's side of the car: names written in stone. On the passenger side is the parking lot for Dundurn Castle, which is now a museum. Meanwhile, the traffic light that has been restraining traffic coming from downtown changes, and the pack of cars in the rearview mirror surges forward. It's hard to be a Sunday driver on the Boulevard: the limit has risen to seventy kilometres an hour, the next set of lights is three kilometres away, and the entrance ramp for a highway is exerting its irresistable pull.

The four lanes of pavement curve one way, then the other, then back again. To the left, a row of conifers stands between road and cemetery. Peering under the canopy of trees to the right, quick glimpses of the bay break through the bush that grows on the steep slope of the Bar, the white triangles of sailboats on the water. The sensation of riding high and narrow over water is not yet strong, but its moment approaches.

And arrives. The trees thin out on both sides, fall away completely, and the sky suddenly opens to the horizon. The Bar narrows to the width of four lanes, the four lanes become a bridge, and for the space of twenty seconds, at posted speed limits, you can take in what might be called the defining view of this place, this westernmost tip of the easternmost Great Lake. *Head of the Lake*, as it was known during Simcoe's tenure. Water, hills, trees, and a city—all framed in the rock embrace of the Niagara Escarpment as the escarpment negotiates a hairpin turn around the end of Lake Ontario. The head, floating above the steering wheel, floating over water on both sides, wants to spin a full three-hundred-and-sixty degrees.

Twenty seconds, then the trees begin to swallow the horizon again.

*I am attached to a piece of geography*—and to the surrounding lay of land. Do you need a permit for this?

# Lay-by

BEYOND THE BRIDGE with its three-hundred-and-sixty-degree view, a small, park-like area appears, where the curb widens away from the road, creating space for parking. The perfect spot to pause on the way to work, or mid-tour.

In a clearing to the left, below the level of the pavement, is a short, rectangular hill; a tumulus. A rock sits atop the tumulus, resting there like a great grey egg. A commemorative egg: attached to it is a plaque. The rock slumps slightly, as though it were slowly being swallowed by the hill.

A line is strung from rock to road. It crosses the four lanes of traffic, threads through the parked car where I am sitting, then runs between the two rows of ceremonial trees on this side of the road, and climbs a wide flight of steps up a second tumulus, a ziggurat of grass, stopping at a blue shield that stands on the ziggurat's flat summit.

The line is purely of my own imagining. I pause to hang or balance on it, between these two short hills, their rock and their shield. A third marker stands at the curb in front of the car. Tall and skinny, it leans over the hood like a teacher over a desk.

P
15 MIN

Whatever happens here will happen within fifteen minutes, the sign seems to suggest.

I HAVE DECIDED TO WAIT and see. During my first five minutes on the line between rock and shield I plan to count cars: both those coming toward me and those going my way—were I going. For the next ten of the allotted fifteen I will keep a running tally of the people who may be walking, jogging or cycling past, note their direction, on which side of the road they're travelling, and, by the digital clock on the dashboard, the minute they pass by the car. I will also keep track of any cars that stop. I will count them here and on the other side, coming and going. I will not overstay my welcome. When the fifteen minutes are up, good citizen-guest will restart the engine and be on his way.

*Lay-by*

Someone's head suddenly hovers over the windshield: a jogger in full jogging regalia, which is not a great deal, and skin-tight, leans over the hood of the car beside the P/15 MIN sign and waves at me, her legs still pumping in rhythm. It takes a long moment for recognition to come—ah, Sheila—and to return the wave. I don't expect to see anyone I know here, acquaintance or friend, and feel vaguely embarrassed.

She lopes off.

9:37 A.M. FEMALE. JOGS NORTH. MARSH SIDEWALK.

# So pleased with this place

SOME LAND FEATURES HAVE event-quality written all over them, you can tell they *happened.* Beyond the lay-by, the road continues to bear right, gently, in the direction of the bay, as though the Bar bellied laterally into the marsh. The Bar does belly, and the bigger waters that shaped this snake of land into a long curve have a hand on the steering wheel.

There *is* something ceremonial about this, the carrying of glacially-transported stones to the meeting place of meltwater stream and lake. Separated by size, the sand and gravel, pebble and cobble were arranged by the two waters into layers, and deposited, one over the other. *With care.* If dance is the engagement of two or more bodies in a ritual activity of proximity and physical contact, that has pleasure written all over it, then this was dance. I take the long-ago clattering of these stones as pure pleasure.

The dance travelled in a northerly direction under the strength of the lake's lead, its clockwise current. The slight curve that translates to the hand on the steering wheel is the sweep of the clock's hand. Where the music stopped is where the waters more recently freed from the glacier entered the water freed earlier, curling around the end of what the two had made together, the body of land that lay between them: the Iroquois Bar. On the day that twelve small stones were deposited on the Bar's beach by the wave of my surprise, involuntary statement in the car, I had only lately learned what I was driving upon, that I was travelling in the same direction as the dance. My twelve are a late contribution, thirteen thousand years or so after the music stopped. I am attached to the dance of the landscape of home.

IT'S QUIETER HERE, NOW. A short, narrow river loops around the end of the Bar, a band of water as calm and retired-looking as the Bar itself. The channel has high shores on both sides. High and steep shores which suggest the activity of those later ice-age days was intense, violent. From the top, especially in winter when the trees that somehow grow on the slope aren't obscuring the view with their leaves, you peer over the edge, and edge back. If it were any steeper, the slope would have to be called a cliff. Or: lay a left arm on the table, palm down; curl the fingers under, into a fist: the drop is as sharp as from knuckles to table.

Come, let us anthropomorphize the landscape. The story here is about bodies—human, liquid, and that one called earth—about where and how they meet, and what happens then. Stories about figures lying under or within land features have been told for centuries. The figures are suggested by the shapes of the landscape itself, and the stories spring both from a sense of belonging and of longing, from love and from loss. They are told in places where the physical and human geography has been changed or damaged. The figure seen in the landscape is usually one who has fought for the place, unsuccessfully. A hero who has lain down, fallen. A sleeping giant, who may one day rise to restore the landscape.

Hope and desire commingle. The living memory of how the place once was is given body, and that body is the earthly home of people for whom the very contours of the land evoke meaning. They are also part of the landscape, those who have lived and died and are buried there. The sleeper keeps alive a connection between place and people that precedes the damage done. It's almost a kind of secret between the two, this kept memory.

Glacial water's handiwork or sleeping giant: take your pick. Have both.

Here, the sleeper is also a visual aid by which to imagine this particular landscape. Someone is lying beside a body of water. This someone stretches large as the Niagara Escarpment across the horizon. He lies upon his left arm, which reaches out diagonally across a beach. The upper half of the arm rests on the sand, where much smaller figures have constructed houses and buildings, a city, tying down this Gulliver with bands of asphalt. From elbow to hand the arm lies half-submerged in water. The hand almost reaches the opposite shore. If the fingers weren't clenched, they would touch it.

Someone is dreaming his own future.

THREE YEARS AFTER HIS FIRST VISIT, Lieutenant-Governor Simcoe called again at the Beasleys' in their log home. The first time, he had come on foot. On this occasion he travelled by boat, over the bay, and was accompanied by his wife, Lady Elizabeth Simcoe. Lady Simcoe kept a diary.

> At eight o'clock we set out in a boat to go to Beasley's, at the head of Burlington Bay, about eight miles. The river and bay were full of canoes; the Indians were fishing; we bought some fine salmon of them.

I am attached to the Lady's diary entry. If it exudes the privilege of her position as wife of the King's representative, it also expresses the sense of privilege she felt on coming into this landscape.

> When we had near crossed the Bay Beasley house became a very pretty object. We landed at it and walked up the hill, from whence is a beautiful view of the lake, with wooded points breaking the line of shore and Flamborough in the background. The hill is quite like a park, fine turf with large Oak trees dispersed but no underwood.

Landscape is so utterly different when it is not populated, or barely so: when it is uncomplicated by a relationship with too many people, over too long a period of time. The first days and years of settlement look, from this distance, like cottage life, gloriously evoking both nature and civilization. The hill Lady Simcoe describes is the slope of the Iroquois Bar and an oak savannah, the mature forest of an arid landscape, its underbrush eaten away by deer or burned in fires that would not affect the thickly armoured trunks.

> We walked two miles on this Park, which is quite natural, for there are no settlements near it.

*So pleased with this place*

If the Lady does not exaggerate, then she and the Governor walked to the very end of the Iroquois Bar. Perhaps they peered over the edge, and edged back. He may have pointed out to her his plans for a military escape route off the Bar, at the marsh entrance of the channel around the Bar's end, with a floating bridge. They may have seen a few boats plying the waters below, since the channel was already a canal route from the lake and Burlington Bay to one of the few towns in the area, Dundas, which lay at the far end of the marsh.

Lady Simcoe drew a number of sketches from various viewpoints on their walk, which accompany the entry in her diary. She recorded an evening walk on the beach with Richard Beasley, where he gave her "a weed, somewhat like a milkwort, a small white flower with a long root, which tastes hot and aromatic, which he called rattlesnake plantain." To mount in her scrapbook. One of the first white settlers, entertaining one of his first guests.

> I was so pleased with this place that the Gov. stay'd & dined at Beasley's.

Events moved quickly after their brief stay. Sixty years later, the "Park ... (with) no settlements near it" that so pleased the Lady had already been conferred city status. During that time the Simcoes' dinner hosts had relocated, twice. The Beasleys' first move was out of their ravine by the bay and into a new, two-storey brick home on top of the Heights. Later, the family experienced a fall from financial grace and were forced to move off Burlington Heights altogether, into a more modest home that stood on the meltwater side of the Bar. Monuments and impressive dwellings aside, however, Richard and Henrietta planted a family tree that has ramified through two centuries. They're still in the phone book.

The new owner of their property, Alexander MacNab, built Dundurn Castle. Burlington Heights, Burlington Bay, and the Flamborough cited in Lady Simcoe's diary entry were all named by Lieutenant-Governor Simcoe after places he remembered in England, places the present landscape evoked for him. Dundurn, on the other hand, was named not from personal memory of a place in Scotland, but from MacNab's dream of that place. He had not yet visited his family's ancestral landholding across the ocean, but that fact only inspired in him a longing to emulate all that he felt such a place meant in terms of personal standing and continuity within the landscape. MacNab saw generations rooted and growing in the country estate that he would build on Burlington Heights.

He began the building in 1832. By 1854, when he was overseeing the final improvements to the completed Dundurn Castle, his *other* dream materialized into reality, as the railway came puffing into view from the far end of the Iroquois Bar.

There were several possible and proposed routes, but MacNab wanted the train to steam into town under his bedroom window overlooking the bay—a vantage from which he could incidentally also watch the Beasley's original log home moulder. And he had the political and financial strength to make it happen, to make steel rails bend to his desire.

The only way to reach the Bar from the opposite shore of the bay was by spanning the natural channel, with its steep sides, that flowed around the end. Normally a wooden trestle bridge would have done the job, but here the gap was closed instead with a bridge of landfill thirty-metres high. Bar and beach became permanently attached, as though the clenched fist of the sleeping giant had released his little finger, which now touched the opposite shore.

It was a railway building age. Within a few years a second line came to town, and the gap was bridged again with landfill. This time the attachment was an index finger. All that remained, then, of the natural channel from the marsh into Burlington Bay was a narrow, landlocked patch of water lying between two dams of earth. That pond is what the Simcoes would see today if they peered over the end of the Bar. It's what you would see from a car crossing the bridge that carries York Boulevard over that same gap, if the bridge's concrete railing didn't block the view. It's what you do see when you stop the car and lean over the rail: a still, elongated pool. The reinforced concrete span of the York Boulevard bridge lofts over the water like an extended middle finger. The only finger still tucked under is the ring.

I am attached to the pried-open fist of a sleeper.

THEY DID IT WITH A CASUAL BRUTALITY, those nineteenth-century railway builders, moving earth, stone and water, forever altering the shapes and contours that glaciers and glacial meltwaters had crafted. They must have felt like gods—gods whose work was matched only by the twentieth century's own re-creating impulse, when the car overtook the train and the construction of limited-access highways began. Today, most places in the country, on the continent—in the world—have seen their geographies re-engineered by railway or highway, or both. Because of its location, the Iroquois Bar, Burlington Heights division, has become a veritable transportation corridor, a horizontal monument to motion, crossed on its marsh side by six lanes of highway and two railway lines, on its bay side by four railway lines, and across its top by four lanes of secondary road.

As a feature of the landscape, the Bar lies largely obscured beneath all this movement, its margins inflated with fill for the beds of rail and road, its fingers unclenched. When a friend first moved to town he thought the public works department had simply dump-trucked a causeway across this western end of the bay. It's true. It takes some geo-sleuthing to see beyond the visible and to unearth the original shapes of the landscape. What's surprising, after all this, is that the shapes still exist. The landscape persists.

THE STORY OF THE NINETEENTH-CENTURY Bar-altering hasn't yet reached its crowning moment, however. When the first earthen dam was built across the original channel, a new channel had to be provided for water to flow into the bay, as well as for boats. The original outlet had formed part of the Desjardins Canal, and the railway owed the canal company an alternate route. The contractor who was already busy tipping landfill across the gap was then hired to dig a channel through the Bar.

The chosen location for this geographical amputation was at the Bar's narrowest point, midway along—halfway between elbow and hand. The spot happens to coincide with the midpoint of the twenty-second, three-hundred-and-sixty-degree view I am privileged to take in on most working days. Eight of those twenty seconds take place on the bridge that spans the open wound of the channel cut, the cut being the only reason a bridge is required. By the luck of the lay of land and water, the railway builders zeroed-in on the very point around which the landscape revolved, and started digging. Looking for the centre of the earth, no doubt.

I come not to praise but to disparage this kind of abuse, but you'd almost think that the landscape itself had a hand, as it were, and if it could, in choosing the spot. Strange enough that the cut sliced through the centre, but over the succeeding century and a half the scene of this violence has actually served to protect the Iroquois Bar as a whole. Each time a new road or railway was constructed, it required a bridge. Six of them span the canal cut today. The cut has become the narrow waist of an hourglass, where all the lines of transportation converge, while the Bar shorelines on either side bulge with the landfill of road and rail bed. Without the cut, the Bar would have become even more inflated and ill-defined than it is.

When the present High Level Bridge was erected in 1932, the rough utilitarianism of the railway was at last introduced to a competing ethic. The modest Art Deco masterpiece of steel and cut stone recognized and enhanced where it stood in relation to the landscape. The year was exactly one century after Alexander MacNab bought the Beasleys' property and started dreaming in steam.

The landscape persists. All it had to do was forfeit an arm.

CRUISING YORK BOULEVARD over the Iroquois Bar. The trees on both sides thin out, the sky opens suddenly to the horizon, and for twenty seconds you can take in the defining view of this area once called Head of the Lake.

What you see in this view from the High Level Bridge is, to the west, Cootes Paradise. Cootes is the smaller body of water—it's a marsh, actually—that would add only ten kilometres to my daily drive to work. It's dotted with several islands,

and has a shoreline of inlets and points, and hills that roll down through Dundas Valley in the distance, hills that stop only at the very edge of the water.

The Niagara Escarpment provides a backdrop to the view. Dundas Valley breaches the escarpment's rock wall with a wide canyon, a gorge that the hills fall over and through as though they were the earthbound version of the Niagara River below the Falls, the water roiling through the high walls. The Dundas Valley hills are, in fact, the memory of a river—a frozen river. They were shaped by the various ice-age glaciers that advanced through the gorge.

The valley is vee-shaped, like a flock of migrating birds. The two escarpment walls come together, though not to a point, as they move west. Standing on the bridge, you are in the empty space between stems of the vee, where the walls of the escarpment have spread ten kilometres apart. In the view from the opposite side of the bridge, the stems open wider. Directly ahead, east, lies Burlington Bay. On each side of the

bay is a terrace of land, and in the middle horizon, a long, low sandbar connects the two terraces, and separates the bay from Lake Ontario. The escarpment walls, spreading away and into the distance on both sides, now seem more like the bell of a trumpet, herald to the rising sun, than simple vee.

*Cootes Paradise*

The landscape as trumpet, held in the broken arm of the Iroquois Bar. And the wind blows through. It's usually westerlies here, and as any jogger, walker or cyclist crossing the bridge, any cormorant flying between its pylons will tell you, the wind blows hardest, loudest, through this canal cut.

The settlement that grew to be a city sits on the terrace to the right, the south, between the escarpment and the bay. It might have remained known as Head of the Lake, or could have been called Burlington, in keeping with both the Heights and Burlington Bay. Instead, it was named after the man who first drew its town plan, early in the nineteenth century. Burlington is now a city on the left side of the bay, farther up the stem of the vee and along the shore of Lake Ontario, while

35

the bay itself was renamed Hamilton Harbour, after the city, early in the twentieth century. The industry with which Hamilton has been identified for the past century occupies about twenty degrees of the three-hundred-and-sixty-degree view. It's in the distance, on the outside curve of the trumpet's bell, downwind. Definitely a part of the view, though, from this end of the city, not defining.

As if to sound a note on the trumpet, a long finger of land, Carroll's Point, extends from the north shoreline of the bay. The finger curls at its tip to face the High Level Bridge, and seems almost close enough to touch. But Carroll's Point is a challenge to reach on foot. I've gone there with family and friends. We've built small fires out of driftwood on the sand, and pretended to be camping at a northern lake. The long hill of sand, gravel, pebble and cobble that Lady Simcoe saw as she entered Burlington Bay lay stretched over the water before us, carrying the vehicles that we could see crossing the bridge, but couldn't hear. It was implausibly quiet, surpris-

ingly private. The first time out, we were so pleased with this place so close to our city homes that we wished we'd brought hot dogs and marshmallows, and stay'd & dined.

It's intimate and broad, this landscape; embracing and open. Debased and persisting. Glaciated countrysides are often more subtle than they are dramatic, as though tamed by the long-term crushing violence of waves of ice. They have a low-key, inviting energy that draws you into their features, folds and cleavages, their rolling roundnesses, into their meetings of land and water. And here, at Head of the Lake, it's all land meeting water. In some ways this meeting place is the opposite of Niagara Falls, which falls over the same escarpment wall that runs through Hamilton, and is part of the same landscape of ice-age effects, but which no one would call subtle. People respond to their landscape, and over time act upon its particular energy, for better, for worse. The Falls is a literal example of people acting upon the energy of a place, but even before the turbines began spinning, before wires alive with

*Carroll's Point*

electricity were slung across the countryside, the nineteenth century was stringing tightrope after tightrope wire across the Niagara Gorge for the daredevils and acrobats who wanted to walk, hop and cycle across. As though, in the face of all that natural power, they had to do *something*.

Before the daredevils, however, honeymooners were attracted to the edge. They were among the first to come, and today you still unfailingly find yourself standing beside the newly wed when you visit. You wonder, what is it about this place that attracts these people? What is it about any place, and the people who settle there for the duration?

# Lay-by

P/15 MIN   (3:55–4:10 P.M.)

3:55–4:00   NINETY-THREE VEHICLES GO BY.

They come in waves released by the traffic lights at either end of the Bar. A wave from one direction, a wave from the other. Sometimes the waves meet, their sounds crashing. It's difficult to count cars that are whipping past in opposite directions, simultaneously, in packs.

4:01   TWO CARS PARKED IN FRONT; ONE PARKED ON BAY SIDE.
4:02   MALE, FIFTY-ISH, COMES WALKING FROM AREA AROUND ROCK, ENTERS CAR IN FRONT, LEAVES.
4:02   CYCLIST, BAY SIDE, HEADING NORTH, MALE, TWENTY-ISH.
4:03   CAR ON BAY SIDE LEAVES; NEW CAR TAKES ITS PLACE.

Someone has to do it, I figure. Someone has to experience at least a little of what this piece of landscape experiences every day.

I am again speaking as if the sandbar is a person. The sandbar is not a person.

| | |
|---|---|
| 4:05 | PICKUP TRUCK, BAY SIDE, FORTIES MALE, WALKS UP ZIGGURAT TO THE LOOKOUT OVER THE BAY, READS BLUE SHIELD. |
| 4:06 | CYCLIST ON SIDEWALK, MARSH SIDE, HEADING NORTH; MALE, FIFTIES, COMES OUT FROM TREES AND ENTERS OTHER CAR IN FRONT OF ME, LEAVES. |
| 4:07 | PICKUP TRUCK MALE LEAVES. |

What does it mean, to share the landscape's experience? Is it possible for the landscape to share?

| | |
|---|---|
| 4:09 | OTHER CAR ON BAY SIDE LEAVES. |
| 4:10 | CAR PASSING BY HONKS, MALE ON PASSENGER SIDE WAVES AND HOOTS; NO ONE I RECOGNIZE. |

# The whole night going on without us

WHAT I LOVE IS THE WAY IT LIES upon the landscape. The long, curving stretch of it. A person would be blind not to recognize the erotic elements, the pure sensuality of its shape held in the liquid embrace of bay and marsh, but this piece of geography, this ice-age sculpture, also takes me back.

I've seen the action of water on sand and stone, and what happens when water meets water. Vacation play as a child often involved halting and redirecting the shallow streams that cut across the beach and entered the lake where we spent our two weeks in the summer. The days found us digging handfuls of sand, using any available piece of driftwood or rock to bulk up the growing dam, and working toward the final, frantic moment of out-rushing the water by throwing sand into the one remaining gap more quickly than the water could wash it away and escape.

The water would slowly pool then, expanding its shoreline behind our earthwork like a balloon filling with air. After a time, it began to overflow its banks, sending flat, investigative snakes to nose for a way around the obstruction. Those passages that the liquid snakes created we blocked with more sand; or we allowed them. Or we dug a new channel and completely rerouted the stream. Or the dam was purposely punctured, in order to watch the stream reclaim the dried badlands of its former bed, and eat our work. It was a game, and a form of competition.

Whatever victory we thought we had won was always short-lived and could never match the quiet relentlessness with which the water would build behind the dam, dooming our efforts to failure. The climax came when the first trickle of water made it over the top, and a quickly widening torrent began to pour through the breach. And our game could never compete with the one that was going on between the stream and the lake, which the stream ran to like a child runs to its parent, not to be stopped.

As we sat around our campfire behind the dunes or slept in the tent trailer, the lake would regularly refashion the beach landscape, erasing the evidence of our day's activity. In the morning we would find the pieces of driftwood and the rocks we had used stranded in the sand, bereft of the purpose we had given them. So much had taken place while we were away. If there had been an overnight storm, even those remnants of our dam might disappear and the configuration of the stream and the sand it flowed over and through would be altered beyond recognition, shaped into new forms that were beautiful and original and complete.

Something was always happening. On the nights of heavy waves, when it sounded as though a landing force had gained the beach with cannons booming, the stream might actually be stopped four or five feet short of the lake. Depending on the angle at which the waves had been hitting the beach, the stream might be forced into a sharp left or right turn, so that in the morning it was running parallel to the shoreline for twenty or thirty feet behind a low dike of sand before the lake finally gave in to the inevitable, and the stream turned and entered it.

It never bothered us to see our hard work washed out, because it was obvious that what was going on was bigger than us. This was their game, the stream's and the lake's, and they could play it any way they wished. There was some comfort in knowing that the water would wash away everything we had done and take over the beach again. We were given a clean slate to start on every morning. True guests, we were treated as though we had no history, only the present. We were allowed that special dispensation of guests to enjoy ourselves. We were even granted the feeling of power.

In the morning we would come upon the scene and feel like time-travellers, visitors from the future, or like those immigrants who return to visit their former homeland only to find it has become somehow foreign. We remained the same, but the landscape had altered. The shapes and forms that we had run over the dunes to see lay there like a living memory of all that could happen over the whole night going on between our departure and our return—going on without us.

## Giants

There used to be giants,
and they loved it here. They'd sit
their giant hinds in a row along the top edge
of the escarpment, and pick at the loose rock
with their hands or their feet, then throw or skip the smoothest
stones across the bay, to see who could land one
on the sandstrip, three miles away;

or they'd spring themselves off the scarp top
like you would off a low wall, and go running
all the way to the end of the sandbar,
then jump across the water to the other side,
or jump in, splashing and yelling up the ravines,
chasing each other's echoes.

This was only a few thousand years ago, and the giants
were still excited about the glaciers,
which were just leaving; about not having to wear
their coats all the time, and what
the ice and water had done, shaping and carving
this gentle, wild landscape!

They loved it here.

I'm telling you, they absolutely loved
every living minute here,

and they regretted ever having to leave.

HEAD OF THE LAKE  *detail on page 65*

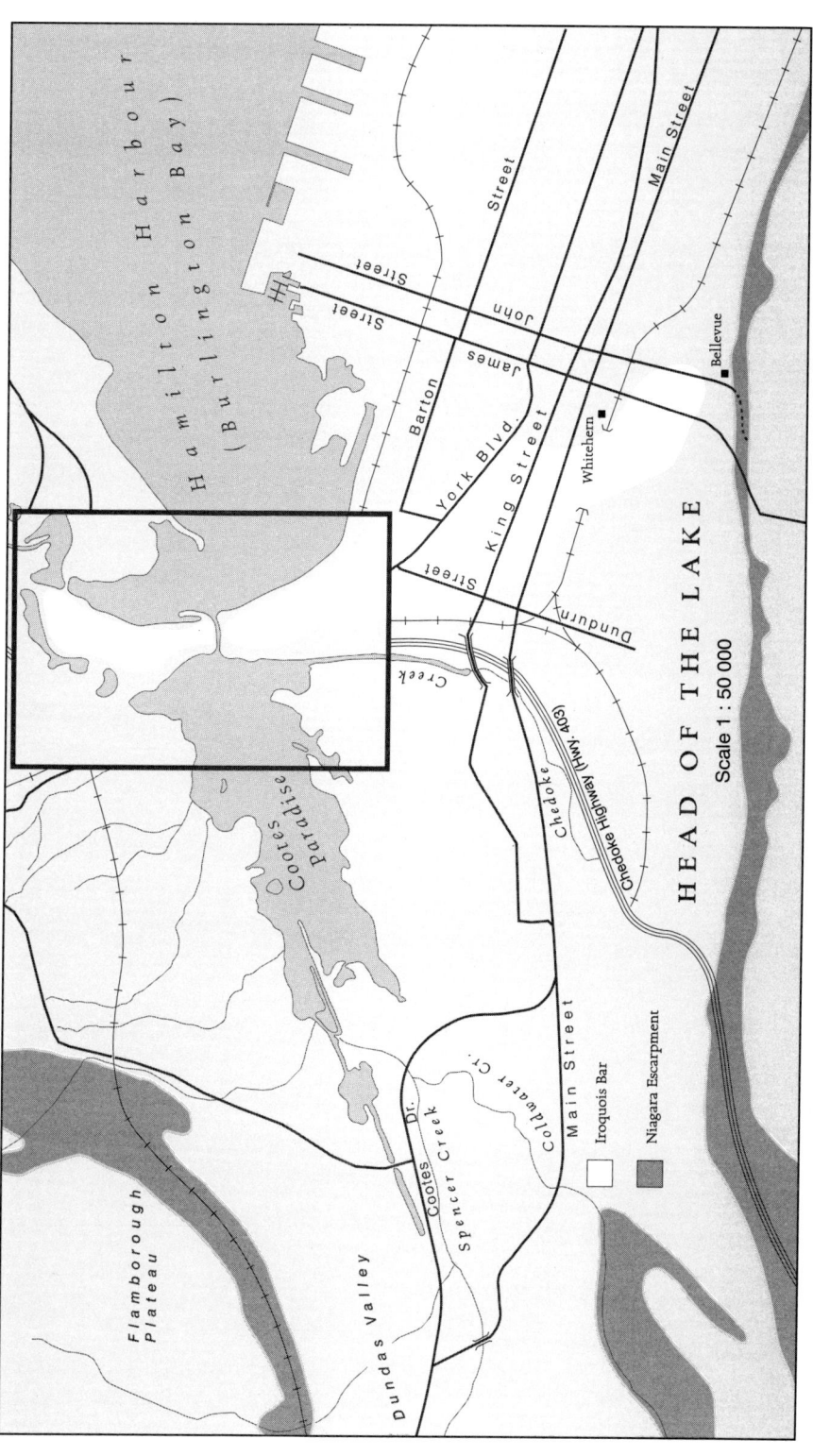

# Lay-by

(5:25–5:40 P.M.)

5:25–5:30    EIGHTY-FOUR VEHICLES, I.E. ONE QUARTER OF ONE PERCENT OF THE TOTAL NUMBER OF VEHICLES THAT CROSS THE HIGH LEVEL BRIDGE EVERY DAY. THREE PARKED CARS: ONE, BLUE, ON THIS SIDE; RED, GREEN, ON OPPOSITE.

5:31    BLUE CAR IN FRONT LEAVES; IMMEDIATELY REPLACED BY SECOND BLUE CAR.

Lost it today. The connection.

It must be here somewhere. Sometime between child and adulthood the unthinking, intimate relation disappeared. Didn't grow or mature with the person. There's been a disengagement from the earth that the child crawled over and touched, was part of. A disconnection, as a boat is disconnected from a dock and moves away over the water, with no reference but the stars above to discover where it is, and only the daily waves and weather to occupy mind and body. That, and its own damn rigging.

This landscape isn't helping. In the library downtown today, looking over old maps and clippings, I realized that not one square inch of the Iroquois Bar has remained untouched, undisturbed; there's not one square inch that hasn't been raked and clawed, dug or filled.

I want my one square inch.

> 5:33      MID-AGE MALE EMERGES FROM BLUE COCOON; WALKS TOWARD ROCK, SLOWLY, HANDS IN JACKET POCKET.
> 5:34      GREEN CAR OPPOSITE LEAVES.
> 5:36      WALKING COUPLE, FEMALE AND MALE, BAY SIDEWALK, HEADING NORTH TOWARD END OF HEIGHTS.

One solitary person, sitting in a car, looking for some solid physical meaning in the time and place he finds himself, as half the population goes like mad in one direction, the other half equally mad in the opposite.

# Motion and Memory

I AM ATTACHED TO A PIECE OF GEOGRAPHY ...

Time to back up a little. Some baggage has barged through the canal under the High Level Bridge, and deserves unloading.

On the day the words first rolled off my tongue into the closed air of the car, I had just driven my wife, Mary, to her place of work and was on the way to mine, planning another fifteen-minute stopover on the invisible line between rock and blue shield. I headed along Barton Street, which runs more or less parallel to the shoreline of the bay until it meets the Bar at the western end of downtown. Just before that point, the street descends a steep hill.

I shouldn't be able to do this, I thought, as I reached the bottom of the hill and after a few blocks began climbing a matching slope on the other side. I should be floating, or sinking. These two hills are the sides of an inlet that once extended a narrow tongue of water into the side of the raised shore on which the city grew. The inlet had been re-landscaped together with the bay shore of the Bar when the railway came to town: its mouth had been landfilled for the track bed. On the day the first train steamed into town, the man in Dundurn Castle, on the hill just beside the inlet, looked down from his bedroom window and watched the train enter a station built on top of that closed mouth.

At the time, the railway's infill did not represent a radical departure from land-use policy. No land-use policy existed. The inlet was on the periphery of settlement, and for some years already had served as the local dump. It seems entirely natural that in a pedestrian and horse-drawn time people would look as near to home as possible for a spot not likely to be built on, a low spot, perhaps a bit marshy, to back their wagons to the lip, and tip. It seems natural, too, for any human settlement that grows into a city to remodel its landscape in this and other ways as it shapes its own geography of houses, buildings and streets. The highs are gradually shaved lower and the lows are slowly filled in. One change is layered upon another. The changes that occur in one generation overlap the changes of the preceding generation in a kind of civic, sedimentary layering. Together these layers become part of the "natural" landscape for the next generation, while the original lay of the land is secreted away underneath. The outside edges of settlement are most susceptible to this reshaping, as is any place where land meets water, where the surface that can be lived upon meets the one that cannot. And here, as we know, it is all land meeting water.

In the long term, however, some changes are more palatable than others. And some days one is better equipped to deal with these changes than on other days. I am Dutch-blooded, a child of immigrant parents, and so the altering of a water-edged environment seems entirely natural to me, but one hundred and fifty years after the deed, the obscured inland reach and the filled mouth of this inlet can still send me over the edge. I launch into a loud rant, alone, in the car—an act that in itself is loaded with irony. A loud rant, followed by a wave of misery that crashes into despair that slips back to the quiet resignation in which I wait at the lights: anger at the cavalier manner in which the landscape has been forever reshaped; misery that I will never lay eyes on the landscape Richard and Henrietta Beasley or John and Elizabeth Simcoe saw in that honeymoon phase of habitation here; and despair over this one small, degraded bit of earth as a sampler for the whole blue ball.

All of this is accompanied by a kind of physical ache. The more I come to know of how the land once lay, the deeper digs the ache. I seek no romantic transport into the natural perfection of the past, but what do you do with your feeling for a place when the changes that are brought to it continually drive home the point that you will be punished for your affection by having its object disfigured or destroyed?

Sigh a resigned sigh at the traffic lights.

AS I DROVE DOWN AND ACROSS the dry inlet on this particular day, the view changed. I saw that in the way the earth fell, bottomed and rose again, it still carried the memory of its original lines. The two-storey, steel-sided factories, the gas station, and the scattered homes all attended to those lines with parking lots that tilted gently toward the bay, with retaining walls, and with basement doors that opened into backyards. Looking toward downtown into what would have been the inlet's furthest reach, I saw an open, sloped area of brown grass. It probably attracted toboggans in winter.

With the slope's dun contours set against the straight lines of the buildings, I found myself thinking of my grandmother, of all people, standing over me in her pale brown cotton dress, framed by a doorway and some furniture, during the one and only time that I saw her: a week or two, when I was very young. She had come to visit us from a country an entire ocean and half a continent away, the place our parents came from too, and one that none of us, her grandchildren, could ever know to any settled depth, no matter how often we might visit there later as teenagers and adults, a place which at some point in our lives we would not be able to think about without some sense of loss. A wonderful, strong person, my grandmother carried within her, within her frame and dignified bearing, many generations of life in Friesland, a northern province of the Netherlands. This piece of landscape I was looking at carried the same long, living memory within itself as she did, and I realized that in the feeling of loss I carried, the two were somehow connected.

The earth remembers. What a thought. The battered earth remembers; on top of which, I shared that memory. By virtue of birth (Dutch-blooded but Canadian-born) and choice of residence, I was inextricably part of the land-filling, refuse-dumping, train-riding, steel-making, car-driving family of earthlings who dwelt here, but by virtue of what a few old maps in the library downtown had shown me, and what I had pieced together driving around, awake to the shapes surrounding me, I was also part of this other relation. Part of how the lines of the slope still curved and climbed, of how they had not forgotten but remained as true as they could to where they first were drawn. It struck me as an act of inordinate kindness, being taken in by these lines, a kind of gentle openness that I also recalled in my grandmother, with whom

I otherwise could not exchange a word. This benevolence, as much as the slope's shape and colour, drew my recollection of her together with the place. It allowed this immigrant offspring a physical connection to where he lived that he'd never experienced before, a connection not earned simply by virtue of having lived at this location for the past twenty years or two generations—or ten generations. It was being given.

Not bad for one lousy patch of godforsaken vacant lot.

And it was happening as I drove by. The remembering was an active event. After all that had been done over the years to alter its shape almost beyond recognition, the earth lay there in its current dress patiently refusing to forget. And I saw this refusal to forget as a kind of resistance. Resistance to whatever would break the spirit, madden the mind, injure or destroy the body. A resistance that is one secret of joy. And I realized that I had joined the resistance.

In the bedtime stories my father told my brother and me, he and others fought underground against the German occupation when the Netherlands was overrun during the war, and though it was a wild stretch to place that experience beside this one, still, two hundred years of settlement can make the landscape appear as though it's been invaded and is under enemy occupation. To resist this occupying power had often felt futile to me, while the pursuit of these lost inlet lines, the lines of stream beds buried under city streets, the obscured lines of the glacial sand-and-gravel bar, had often become an exercise in melancholia.

But here, now, the earth's own substantial memory was giving its silent affirmation, where I least expected it, as it had been all along.

AFTER CLIMBING THE FAR SIDE of the inlet I was soon turning onto York Boulevard, passing under the traffic lights, beyond Dundurn Castle and the cemetery, and crossing the Iroquois Bar. The words began to formulate, *I am attached* ....

A person may often experience even the most familiar landscape only from the inside of a car, at a certain number of kilometres an hour, as scenery. That's how I and thirty-five thousand others daily experienced this one. Any attachment to the world scrolling by the car window is largely aesthetic, as brief as traffic conditions and the speed limit allow. The hand upon the steering wheel our only touch; our only taste, the drink steaming in a cup holder.

When the car stops and a foot emerges, though, the familiar downward pull exerts itself and proves the attachment is also literal. The second foot follows, the door is slammed shut, and the feet then take turns touching down and lifting off. A rhythm is played between this literal, inescapable attachment to the earth that all legged creatures share, and the freedom of movement that keeps us from growing roots. A dance, between our bodies and the body of earth.

The first time I emerged from my car and intentionally set foot upon this piece of geography was in the cemetery across the street from Dundurn Castle: the long narrow burial ground between York Boulevard and the marsh slope of the Iroquois Bar. I wanted to know if a land feature that was so decidedly a transportation corridor could also be a place, however that term might be defined. If it could still be itself.

The time was mid-November, the weather appropriately damp, cold and windy, with occasional volleys of frozen rain. Why would anyone choose to live in a place with weather like this? Or take his family out on a day like this? The wind blew the fallen leaves against the tree trunks and gravestones, and, together with the clattering pellets of rain, almost succeeded in drowning out the sound of traffic from the road: half the population going like mad to get some place else, the other half forever staying put.

The narrow roads wandered around the site as aimlessly as suburban streets. Reading inscriptions as we ducked along, the three of us—father, mother, daughter—saw stones incised with family names still familiar in the city, descendant from the original settlers. Beasley. Land. Gage. Mills. At one point, the road we were walking curved and met a long, narrow hill, a miniature version of the Iroquois Bar, laid crosswise over the Bar. A number of elaborate crypts were built into it. The road swept past these, turned sharply and cut directly through the hill. Set into the shoulder of the cut was a low, bevelled stone marker:

> THESE RAMPARTS WERE
> ERECTED BY THE BRITISH TROOPS
> DURING THE WAR OF 1812–13
>
> FROM THIS PLACE ON THE NIGHT
> OF JUNE 5, 1813
> 700 MEN UNDER THE COMMAND
> OF LIEUT. COLONEL HARVEY
> MARCHED TO STONEY CREEK
> WHERE THEY SURPRISED AND ROUTED
> AN AMERICAN FORCE OF 3750 MEN
> RIDDING THE NIAGARA PENINSULA
> OF THE INVADERS

Governor Simcoe had it right. Seventeen years after the two couples dined, the Americans invaded. A war had been fought, and Burlington Heights played a part in producing victory for our side. Nice to know someone considered the place worth fighting for.

"*From this place ...*" From the first moments of my setting foot on it, this overridden piece of geography began declaring itself as just that, a place. A certain kind of place. The marker from the War of 1812 that we bumped into that day was the first of many that I soon found scattered all over the Heights, as though the cemetery was colonizing the landscape beyond its borders.

Across the road a cannon pointed over the bay, token of the same War of 1812, two centuries ago. Close by the cannon, beside Dundurn's parking lot, a big stone stood upright honouring Richard and Henrietta Beasley and all the United Empire Loyalists who first settled at Head of the Lake after being driven from their homes before, during and after the Revolutionary War in the United States. Perhaps that's why people chose to live in this place of grey, pelting ice: they had no choice. The stone mentioned the Simcoes' dinner with the Beasleys—a convivial variation on those ubiquitous plaques in the eastern American states with their "George Washington slept here."

Halfway to the High Level Bridge, a slim stone obelisk, six feet tall, marked Mile 17 of the Around the Bay Road Race, a foot race first run in 1894, two years before the Boston Marathon, and still held each spring. Just before the bridge, a stone similar to the first marked where a second line of defense was erected in 1812, at the most easily defended location—the narrowest section of the Bar. I found the idea of retreating farther and farther out onto the long plank of the Iroquois Bar appealing.

A plaque attached to one of the stone pylons of the High Level Bridge commended the politicians and builders behind the bridge's recent reconstruction. While having a few lamps fixed, I later happened to fall into conversation with an almost-retired Mr. Mills, of Mill's Lighting Warehouse (since closed for business) who said that he'd made the original plaque. When that plaque was first installed, one of the designers instructed the workers to unzip their flies and relieve themselves against it, so that the brass would be burnished to a warm glow by the acid in their stream.

The mementoes kept coming. On the other side of the bridge a small, turtle-shaped rock (since replaced by a taller, standing rock) sported a small slab of bronze:

DEDICATED TO FOUNDING LANDSCAPE ARCHITECT
MATTIAS (MATT) BROMAN 1895–1989
WHO SHARED HIS VISION OF THIS GREAT LANDSCAPE

It named that area of Burlington Heights the Broman Lands. Beyond Matt's rock was the short grassy ziggurat to which one end of my imaginary line was connected. The blue shield overlooking the bay honoured one Thomas B. McQuesten, lawyer, city alderman, provincial politician. Another visionary of this great landscape.

Across the road, the stone slowly sinking into the tumulus was dedicated not to a single person or event but to three groups of unidentified people: soldiers from the War of 1812, the victims of ship-fever in 1847, and the immigrants who died during their Atlantic crossing, or soon after, in the two cholera epidemics that struck the city in the first half of the nineteenth century. They lay buried beneath the stone, in mass graves. "*Guard this Resting Place.*"

Farther on, another large stone, with a plaque on either side: one for the first bridge that spanned the end of the Heights in 1921, another for the one that replaced it in 1972.

Then a millstone, set on its edge and wrapped in a steel band to keep its broken pieces together, with a plaque to George Washington Johnson, a local schoolteacher and the author of the nineteenth-century popular song, "When You and I were Young, Maggie."

> *I wandered today to the hill, Maggie,*
> *To watch the scene below ...*
> *The green grove is gone from the hill, Maggie ...*
> *The creaking mill is still.*

A mishmash of markers and memories. The Heights was awash with them, with reminders of those who took up arms on it, fled to it, lived on it, dined on it, ran over it, peed on it, shared visions of it, built roads and bridges, fought and died over it, arrived, became ill and died on it, became old, died, and lay down in it, and sang.

JOHNSON'S SONG IS A FAIRLY COMMON nineteenth-century lament over things passing. But then, his century opened onto a lightly settled landscape of farms, orchards and stone mills, and closed on a city, railroads and the beginnings of heavy industry: some of the population understandably felt a little overwhelmed. Johnson's lyric was published in 1864, a decade after the arrival of the first train, and set to music two years later, whereupon it climbed to the heights of popularity as sheet music. A famous son. Hence the stone.

The millstone memorial was one of the few that had nothing directly to do with Burlington Heights itself, but driving the length of York Boulevard on the morning of my inlet epiphany, I began wondering why it was that so many memorials were attracted to this three-kilometre stretch of the glacial Iroquois Bar, and Maggie gave me a clue.

A huge civic celebration had taken place in the last year of the nineteenth century, when Dundurn Castle was purchased by the city and the estate opened as a park. Another big party was held thirty-three years later with the opening of the High Level Bridge, when most of the remaining Heights became parkland. A feeling of the landscape being reclaimed was in the air, and that the landscape needed reclaiming. Most of the memorial markers were erected during those thirty-some years, each one a claim staked on the place as forever set aside and remembered, inviolable as the gravesite of a loved one. The cemetery *was* colonizing, but in this case the death being commemorated was that of the immediate landscape over the preceding one hundred years.

Geography and population dictated that the Heights was, and ever would be, a transportation corridor, since no other approach led into the city from the north, and the markers were a tacit acknowledgement of that fact. They assumed a kind of perpetual motion, as grave markers assume the living are moving among the dead. These markers stood as brief stone moments of stillness and recollection for a population otherwise on the fly, the walk or the run. It's as though people had learned the hard way that forward motion, or progress, always carried with it the possibility and threat of forgetting:

the forgetting of events, of people and accomplishments, epidemics and death, and also of *where you are*: where you are in relation to what is now invisibly in the past, and where you are literally, in your body, in "this great landscape." Which is why George Johnson sang his sad song, to such a large audience.

By the time the festivities were over and the bridge was opened for traffic, the place had been pared down to its essentials. The houses, billboards, gas station and motel had all vanished, the boathouses clustered around the Desjardins canal cut had mostly been removed or bulldozed, and people no longer dwelt anywhere on Burlington Heights, other than within its sand and gravel, pebble and cobble. What remained were road and markers: a three-kilometre tribute to motion and memory stretched over the water in a kind of high-wire tension.

*The sandbar itself is memory*, I realized: the memory of the motion of streams and waves and currents.

The Iroquois Bar as memory. I thought I heard the landscape hum: wind over high-wire. This took things one giant step beyond the rapture at the inlet on Barton Street. There the earth remembered, was remembering, its original shape. Here, the piece of geography itself was memory.

Then another giant step, as I realized that not only was the Bar itself memory, it was also *made* of memory. The innumerable grains of sand, the gravel, pebble and cobble; each one was a souvenir of glacial travels, a memento of some place else. Memory was layered on top of memory, making memory, in the run and crest of time. The mishmash collection of markers placed on Burlington Heights was only following the lead of what lay beneath the markers, imitating nature, adding a current level to the carefully arranged layers of the natural process.

The humming grew louder.

In a glaciated countryside, the entire landscape is shaped and sculpted on the crest of motion, and has been reshaped and re-sculpted by successive waves of glaciers and their meltwaters. The kneaded earth is kneaded again into hills and troughs. Tons of stone debris are transported here, then there. Beaches and sandbars built by the waves of a glacial lake are drowned or exposed an age later by the next lake. The meltwater torrents of one glacial age carve ravines through the deep clay deposits of the previous. The effects of the last ice age lie upon and interweave with those of other ice ages, creating and recreating land features—and the detectives of physiography have field days.

On the grand scale the same story is true for rock, but the events that form rock are so deeply in the past they stagger the imagination. The work of ice-age water, frozen and free, is relatively recent. Living memory. You can almost hear the crushing, dripping, trickling, coursing, raging shaping of the landscape. At Niagara Falls, it's still happening.

The inlet on Barton Street carries and clings to the memory of its original lines, which are memory, broken and overlaid with the lines of the past two hundred years, which are also memory. And then I recalled my grandmother again, for there was something about her that also suggested a time frame that stretched before and after, of which she embodied the deep present moment as it carried her toward and past me—and I looked up, a small boy just learning to tie his shoe, caught in his own torrent.

BURLINGTON HEIGHTS  *detail on page 113*

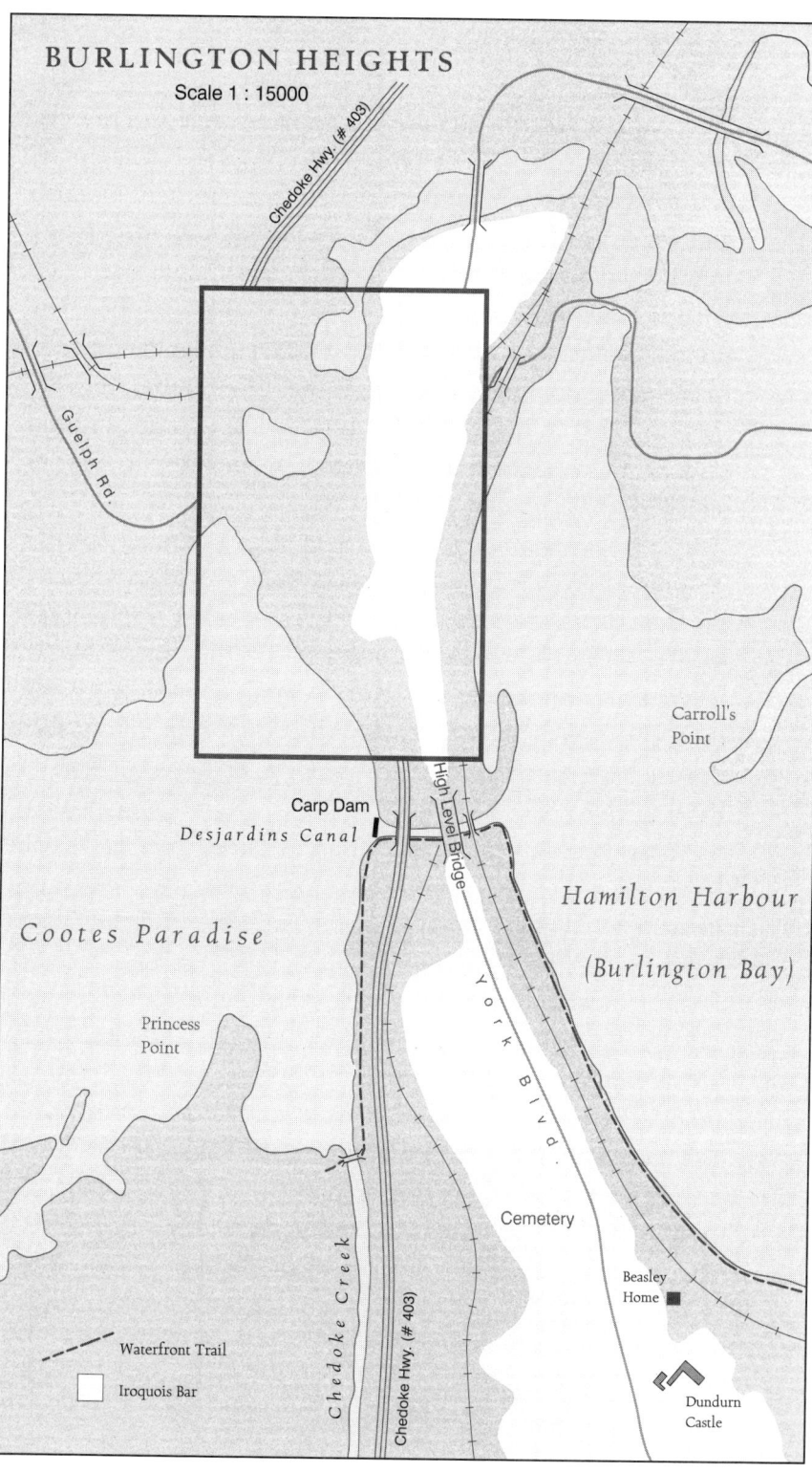

Driving across the Heights that day, I was lost in the daydream of this long hill stretching over the water. The dream had something to do with motion and memory, with earth and water and forgetfulness. The words began to form in my mind: I am attached to how the lines are drawn here. *Geo graphis*. I am attached to what is written. Inlet, shoreline, bar, ravine. I am attached to what the whole night going on without us has accomplished, to what the water and earth have done together, and done again. I am attached to what has been undone, unravelled, to the redrawn, remembering lines. I am attached to this pursuit of them.

It seems hugely unfair that when we go looking for the restoration and reconnection that Nature provides, we head for the unsullied wilds as far away as possible from where we live. After two hundred years of dwelling upon and altering the landscape to suit our changing requirements and economic urgencies, it's as though the earth beneath our feet doesn't have much to offer us anymore, or to tell. It doesn't have much to offer *with*. What it would tell we might rather not hear. We're so used to the one-way street, to being at the receiving end of the relationship, that we feel a sense of entitlement. A landscape relatively untouched by human hand has the gift still to spoil us.

But in my daydream I was beginning to imagine there may actually be more to receive, and to give, here where the Bar's arm lies broken and the bodies are buried, where the inlet's mouth is closed and landfill meets the saddened water, than can be dreamt of on starry nights by northern lakes.

*I am attached to a piece of geography*, in an urban setting. A simple, declarative statement, ending in a term of earth science. I am attached to a feature of the landscape that, like much of the landscape of human habitation, has been treated largely as a material object, a means to an end, but that persists as a still, moving centre, the possible bridge of reciprocity between myself and the physical body on which I dwell. I, too, exist as a feature of this landscape; a moveable feature, granted, but a feature all the same. The same tension of motion and memory exists within me. When I stop, I will join the lines that enthral me now, and what the water leaves behind when it retreats from the shoreline of my physical being will become a part of the landscape as I enter the memory of earth.

But not yet. Beneath the words of my automotive declaration is a barely subdued enthusiasm for this very particular place. A certain contrariness is at work too, because of all places on earth this one is said to defy all natural enthusiasms. Let me add an apology. I apologize in advance for any unpredictable, embarrassing behaviour on my part, possibly in public. I'm thinking, dance. I begin to understand the drumbeat of native dances, which seems to rise from the ground below the feet to enter the rhythm of our walking attachment to it. I may fall in with whatever rhythms the celebrants were stepping lively to in 1932 at the opening bash for the High Level Bridge.

Or I may vocalize. I may reclaim the rights of childhood and yodel my affections like the twelve-year-old boy Mary and I heard shortly after we moved here twenty years ago. When she and I were young.

We were walking along a trail at the bottom of one of the many mini-Niagara Falls in Hamilton that, like the big one, have taken their millennia to gnaw narrow gorges into the wall of the escarpment. This particular set of falls was named after an English vision of paradise, Albion, which Head of the Lake evoked in the minds of the Loyalist settlers. A mill had been located here during the nineteenth century. Because of the mill, the hill of the escarpment, the changes that have occurred to it and to the view below in the years since, I'd come to associate the place, correctly or incorrectly, with the one in George Johnson's song.

The singsong declamation came from somewhere behind us, and as we turned we saw him, the twelve-year-old, accompanied by two friends who sat with their legs dangling over the edge of a rock halfway up the escarpment. He was standing on the lip of the overhanging rock in the spray of descending water, his arms stretched wide, as he sang it out,

"I love you Albion Falls."

Then sang it out again.

# Lay-by

(4:15–4:30 P.M.)

BETWEEN 4:15 AND 4:20, EIGHTY-FIVE VEHICLES GO BY.

4:20      THREE WALKERS, TWO ON OTHER SIDE, STRIDING THE SIDEWALK; ONE ON THIS SIDE; ALL HEADING SOUTH INTO TOWN; ONE CAR IN FRONT OF ME, TWO BEHIND.

4:21      CAR BEHIND PULLS OUT AND AWAY, SINGLE MALE.

Warm, mild, but windy. Buffeting. Sitting in a car stopped on a long hill.

The earth as memory. Memory and event. This place as taking place, shaped and sculpted on the crest of motion, the motion of water; water in all its forms, frozen and free.

What is water, then?

4:22      FRONT CAR PULLS OUT AND AWAY,

SINGLE MALE; SIDEWALK CYCLIST,
BAY SIDE, HEADING SOUTH.

The sound of a train passing. A siren from the highway. This is NOT PEACEFUL.

Perhaps water is time. Time moving with interminable, crushing slowness; coming in waves, rushing in torrents. Washing over or through a person, or carrying them down, down, down, the moment they step into its current.
Giving shape to the days.

| | |
|---|---|
| 4:25 | ANOTHER SIREN FROM THE HIGHWAY. |
| 4:26 | MALE CYCLIST, ON THE ROAD, THIS SIDE, HEADING SOUTH; SIDEWALK CYCLIST, MALE, BAY SIDE, HEADING NORTH. |

Sea plane lands on the harbour. Deafening. Silence. Sitting in a car on a bar in a slow motion through time.

| | |
|---|---|
| 4:27 | FOUR GIRLS, AGES 8–15, BAY SIDE, WALKING NORTH; THEY STOP ON TOP OF THE LOOKOUT, READ THE SIGN, WALK ON. |
| 4:29 | CAR STOPS BEHIND, SINGLE MALE; EMPTIES CONTENTS OF SMALL PLASTIC FLASK INTO GAS TANK, DRIVES OFF. |
| 4:30 | ONE CAR REMAINS. |

# Oriah Mountain Dreamer

*Bring a cushion to sit on, and a candle with
a holder and a plate to catch wax drips.*

MY DAUGHTER AND I WALKED through the front doors of the Omega Centre, past shelves and displays carrying books and related paraphernalia geared to pilgrims of spiritual journeys of every persuasion, and made our way toward the big room at the back of the store. We paid our five dollars and looked for a place to put our cushions. Warning lights had already begun to flicker inside my head.

Together, the two of us had gone to a number of different ceremonies and worship services over the past year, to satisfy her curiosity and my own, and in an attempt to find one that integrated mind, body and spirit without being, at the same time, either boring, removed from the world, or goofy.

We'd attended a Taizé service, a very simple affair of reading and singing with a small group of people, children included, clustered around candles in the forward section of a large, darkened church like the few, happy survivors of a great cataclysm. The effect could only have been enhanced if the building itself had been in ruins. Taizé is a place in France, and the approach to worship developed there had spread throughout the world. We'd sat at the back to maintain our observer status, a contradiction in terms for a service that requires personal presence, and ultimately the service lasted longer than either of us could sit still.

We'd also attended an Anglo-Catholic service on Holy Saturday, the day between Good Friday and Easter, as the lights were gradually extinguished and the building became completely darkened. Then, from a single hidden source at the back, one candle was re-lit and the flame was distributed candle to candle, person to person, until the whole building was ablaze at 12:01 a.m., the first moment of Easter morning. Theatre of the holy. I loved it. Unfortunately, the overwhelming atmosphere of incense made my daughter physically ill.

There were other places and other observances, but all told, our assignment wasn't an easy one. Airdropping into foreign religious landscapes on reconnaisance missions doesn't allow for a very deep exploration, and isn't entirely fair to these landscapes' spiritual integrity. But my daughter was in her year of transition from child into the beginnings of her own personhood, age twelve, so I welcomed her curiosity and willingness.

I was also a bit desperate. The church that we as a family attended was travelling through a patch of misery that would try anyone's childlike faith, and there had already been adult casualties. But I was also naturally ambivalent toward my Judaeo-Christian, Protestant upbringing and bent, simply because it came delivered within an institution that as often as not suppressed as many spiritual instincts as it inspired. The religious tradition I was raised in seemed to me to have almost nothing to say on how a person should relate to their natural environment, their landscape—nothing explicit, in any event.

Rather, it almost bred an antagonism toward the earth, in the same way that it, and other traditions, have bred an antagonism toward the body.

I'd found myself on a narrow, wandering path, and though the path still took me to the appointed place each Sunday-in-the-morning, I did not as a father want to lose my child to her own rapidly-growing self without feeling that she had somehow been touched by the invisible.

We entered the big square room where the Winter Solstice Ceremony was to be held. There were as many levels of concrete layered above us, heading skyward, as there were going down, augered into the earth in descending ramps and parking levels. We'd travelled into the heart of a big city, a city ten times larger than our own, for something the piece of paper I'd received in the mail from a friend claimed had its roots in native American religions.

*Together we will dream the marriage of Sohotomah (Grandfather Sun) and Ehotomah (Grandmother Earth) in the womb of the night.*

Only one open space remained along the walls of the room for us to place our two cushions. A little suburb of someone else's cushions lay beside it. Stationed in front of these cushions were a number of candles in holders, along with small bowls of what looked like incense, and a good-sized portable radio. Two attendants sat on either side of the suburb, two boys, about ten and thirteen, the only non-adults other than my daughter to attend.

Hard furnishings were non-existent in the room, except for a large drum that stood knee-high, a metre and a half across, on wheels, and the small table by the door where our five dollars had been collected. Beside the cash box on the table, stacked copies of a book written by the person who would be leading the ceremony, Oriah Mountain Dreamer, were available. The book was called *Adventures of a Spiritual Thrillseeker.* I have a very sensitive early warning system. Oriah's name had caused a few lights on the control panel to flicker, as did the trappings of the Omega Centre. The title of the book lit up a few more.

Attend without prejudice, I told myself.

We settled in as comfortably as we could as the room began to fill up, mostly with women: of the eighty or so people who eventually filled the room, only ten were male. A woman in a long black dress was walking around the room, talking to various people. It became obvious she had an involvement in the ceremony soon to begin, but I didn't clue in to the fact that the suburb of pillows beside us belonged to her, or that she was Oriah, until the friend who had invited us to the evening arrived and said, "Wanted to get close to the action, did you?" The two young male attendants were Oriah's sons.

THE CEREMONY BEGAN with drumming and singing. Three women sat around the stretched surface of the drum, each with a soft-headed mallet, and went at it, starting off slowly and gradually picking up the pace. They pounded one note in unison and began to sing a rhythmic, tuneless chant. We joined the singing. Chants, in my small experience, are medieval, monastic, and more directly spiritual, even cerebral. This, on the other hand, was decidedly physical. And loud.

I began to imagine that we were sitting on the skin of the earth, a skin stretched taut, and that with each rhythmic boom we all bounced slightly. This, while sitting on carpet-covered concrete. Something about the drumming and chanting recalled the prairie landscape I had grown up in. This is exactly what I'm looking for, I thought, or rather, felt. I flicked off a few of the lights on the panel.

While the drumming and singing continued, everyone in the room was smudged. Oriah had earlier called for volunteers, and I later deduced that she and the other women who participated in this ceremony were members of the DreamStar Lodge. All the members of the lodge were women. Oriah took the ceramic bowl in front of her and pinched some sweet grass into it from a pouch, along with other dried grasses, and then lit it. Once the grass began to smoke it only needed occasional prompting from her lighter, a miniature flame-thrower.

The other members of the lodge imitated each of Oriah's movements, and then, their small bowls smoking, approached the people in the room one by one. Using a bird's wing about the size of a hand, they fanned the smoke directly at, above and on either side of each of us, ceremoniously, and since there were so many of us, swiftly. The smell of the smoke was high summer and the tall dry grass of the prairies, but sweeter.

By this time, all my lights had dimmed and the control board was dark. This was ritual food for spirit and sense, and it came from an earth we knew and lived upon. It wasn't divorced from our physical reality. That what we were doing was a version of a native ceremony, conducted and attended solely by non-natives, I took to be just another of the irreconcilable, odd facts of life in the big city, life on the cusp of a new millennium. And left it at that.

After the smudging, the drumming ended and the pipe

ceremony began. The five women sat in a half-circle around Oriah, and each unpacked and assembled a long-stemmed pipe. Oriah addressed a prayer to the "sacred ones"—the grandmothers and grandfathers, the ancestors. With each statement or request she placed a pinch of tobacco in the pipe. When she was done she would say, "This is what we ask." All six women lit their own pipe and drew on it, facing in the direction in which the prayer was addressed. Oriah then tapped her pipe on the bowl a few times in rapid succession, and began the next prayer. The prayers were addressed to the four directions, West, North, East and South, each of which represented the home or source of the will, the mind, the heart, the spirit.

After she and the others had gone through the four points of the compass, they proceeded into the compass divisions: northwest, southwest, southeast, west northwest. It went on. There are many subdivisions to the direction of prayer. Oriah helped matters along by moving as smoothly and efficiently through this liturgy as any minister or priest I have witnessed moves through his or hers, but this was altogether too similiar to what we, as children in church, used to refer to as the Long Prayer.

The Long Prayer was protracted enough in church, but a few of my friends were obliged to sit through domestic versions before dinner, as their food offered up its smells to their bowed heads and noses. On some level it was impossible to avoid the conclusion that this was a kind of punishment for having a body that required, and desired, sustenance; for having a body at all. It's impossible to deal with this when you're a kid, at home or at church, so a familiar coping mechanism often kicked in then, as it did now. I found myself doing what I had learned to do so well: disconnect and drift. Daydream.

Anticipating this response, Oriah had told us earlier not to feel obliged to take in every word, but to allow the words to wash over us if that should happen. I silently thanked her. If our childhood ministers had said something similar it might have saved some of us from an often resentful guilt, and encouraged us to enter into prayer by another door, a door not attended solely by words.

One of the saving graces of the evening was this complete lack of solemnity or self-importance. Oriah refused to take herself too seriously. A broad swath of humour cut through the evening, self-deprecating to the point of making the self entirely inconsequential to the proceedings, but without the loss of any personal, human dignity. It reminded me of the novels of a few native writers I've read. The trait had seemed particular to them. But I hesitate. Who's reminding whom of what, here? Who owns, and who's borrowing? Was there really any legitimacy to these solstice proceedings?

A slightly programmatic feel began to invade the evening after the prayers, as though we were being offered samples from a larger menu. It was a menu: the evening was offered partly as an introduction to the DreamStar Lodge and alternative spiritual possibilities, directed particularly at women. Native traditions provided the source for most of what we had done thus far, and though warning lights had tentatively flickered a few times during the ceremonies, my comfort level was still high.

After the pipe ceremony, Oriah told us to get comfortable,

lie down if we could—quite a feat in that crowded room—while she led us in a guided dreaming. We positioned ourselves on the floor beside each other like immigrants on a boat to the New World as she slipped a tape into the tape deck beside her. Music began to spill from the speakers. We lay next to each other in the cargo hold as the sound of stringed and wind instruments washed over us, from the opposite end of the musical spectrum as the earlier drumming. With music so lullingly hypnotic—or manipulative—you have to trust the person you're following, and be willing. I guess I lacked both qualitites. As a result, I could not be guided. I remained in the hold as Oriah imagined and guided the other travellers up beyond the planets to wander among the stars.

Someone, she said, a presence of some kind, would come to each of us individually and lead us into another part of the stars where we would be shown the significant events that had happened to us during the year. After the review we would be led back to the meeting place, but before we were left to return to ourselves lying below deck, we would be given words of direction by this presence.

When all had returned from their dreaming adventures and were sitting on their pillows again, Oriah wanted to do one more thing before we left: a blessing. It seemed more like church all the time. She told us we would each need a partner and that our partner should be a person we didn't know. Everyone coupled off quickly, but I was feeling a bit separated from the group now, left on my own shores, and when she asked who didn't have a partner I had to raise my hand along with two others on the opposite side of the room.

The two others found each other right away. The friend who had invited us said later that in Oriah's words nothing "just happens" at a ceremony. What didn't just happen was that Flickering Warning Lights found himself partnered with Oriah Mountain Dreamer. She would bless me and I her.

We sat cross-legged, facing our partner and taking turns with the blessing. Oriah went first, and instructed those who were also going first to place their hands on the floor and breathe in, slowly and deeply. They were to imagine the energy from Grandmother Earth coming up into their body with each inhalation. Even though we were sandwiched between layers of concrete, she said, the earth was still there, somewhere below.

After a number of breaths, she cupped her hands in front of her face and breathed into them. She told the others to imagine their breathing-out as a ball forming in their hands, and instructed them to place their hands on their partner's head, as she placed hers on mine and ran them slowly over my shoulders and arms and to the floor, hands full of the energy from the earth. At the same time she silently intoned my name. Once, twice, three times.

When my turn came to bless Oriah, I found that imagining the energy of Grandmother Earth coming up through our bodies was too abstract. I had to locate myself in an actual place. I flew around, looking for a spot, and in my bird's-eye-view the whole long stretch of the Iroquois Bar began to take shape below me. Surprise. My coasting, hovering seagull was in no hurry. It panned the length, focused and zeroed in on the exact spot it wanted to land.

Once settled, I could imagine Grandmother Earth coming up through my hands placed on her concrete blanket. I could imagine my own grandmother's hand on my head as I successfully tied that shoe. And I could also imagine placing my hands on the head, shoulders and arms of Oriah Mountain Dreamer, which I did.

"What did you think?"
"I loved it," my daughter said as we got in the car. "I want to go again."

She was blessedly free of warning lights, of course, and had no problem at all with the guided dreaming. A little man came up to her among the stars, she said. He had taken her by the hand and shown her movies of her birthday party and of the Hallowe'en party that she and her friends, but mostly she, had organized and successfully pulled off. Before he left he gave her three instructions: be more willing, be more generous, and ... She'd forgotten the third. She liked her little man. He seemed like a brother to the Wizard of Oz.

On the way out of the city we stopped at a variety store to stock up for the drive home. As we crossed the street the wind, which had been blustering all evening, was making a big racket, trying to force a metal garbage can it had worked into the middle of the deserted intersection to get to the other side. It shoved and pushed at the can with repeated blasts, hitting one side, then the other. Taking the part of the can, my young veteran of forays into differing spiritual landscapes joked,

"I'm going, I'm going. Don't worry. I'm getting there. You don't have to keep pushing."

Father and daughter laughing all the way through the doors of the 7–11.

# Ceremony

Some ceremony is involved
in hauling the bicycles up from the basement,
angling their awkwardnesses under
ductwork, around the stairwell landing,
and through the needle's eye of the side door,
as one wheel spins free, ticking.

The sun was singing down, loud and glorious,
as we wove our two thin tire lines through town
and to the bay, then through and around surprising
numbers of walkers, strollers, roller-
bladers of varying degrees of proficiency, and other
cyclists, all of us twisting and braiding
our various momentums together
like a fat rope played out by the water's edge;

and the gravel swallowed our tires as we left the paveway
and headed toward the point, while volleyed in
and out of hearing on the wind
we heard the beat of some hydraulic jack
driving pilings into the earth,

or some jack's boom box, I said,

but came upon the backs of three white
t-shirts there instead, and the draped jet
hair and braids of two men and a woman
sitting facing the open blast

furnace of light on the water,
in the sky, and drumming
the sun down,
singing rhythmic undulations over
the chanted surface of the bay,

a song that went nowhere, musically,
and could have gone there forever—
                                            and the gravel
swallowed our tires again, as we quit
the landfill point to be home before dark,
and all I wanted to convey is the deep enjoyment
of our early summer evening ride, the unexpected
explosion of people at the new waterfront park
three generations after industry and E.coli
drove them all away, and the three first-peoples,
this late in the game, chanting and drumming
the sunset as an event
in which they were participant,
as we looked on.

# Head of the Lake

FOR THE PAST FEW WEEKS Mary and I have been doing the Simcoe thing. Two hundred years later, and inching closer by the day to its anniversary, we are doing what Lieutenant-Governor John Graves and Lady Elizabeth Simcoe did the day they came calling. We are walking the length of Burlington Heights, one end to the other, and back again; the same walk that prompted the royal-representative couple to invite themselves to dinner with the Beasleys.

Each morning we park the car in the lot of Dundurn Castle above the ravine where the Beasley house stood. The log home on the shoreline of the bay, the wharf, the warehouse and other outbuildings that existed at the time have long ago gone the way of untended wood, but precisely dug, rectangular holes have been punctuating the ground lately, and archaeologists are looking for rotted posts and other signs of foundation, as well as for any dropped, tossed or lost articles that once were part of the lives lived here. From the top of the ravine we can just make out the diggings through the leaves.

We move at a brisk clip. The novelty of these daily walks, which are partly physical exercise, partly an exercise in doing something as a couple, and partly an exercise in *being there*, in body, and planting our feet over every square inch of the Iroquois Bar, hasn't yet worn off. Just beyond the High Level Bridge today a lost or tossed object was lying at the side of the on-ramp for the highway. I almost picked it up: a naked, plastic doll.

"What does *that* mean?" Mary asked.

I assumed she was asking after the Meaning, but all she wanted to know was how a naked baby doll came to be lying beside the on-ramp for the highway. What was the rest of the story? What about the young child to whom the doll probably belonged? We stood there for a silent moment, then moved on, letting the baby lie.

Our daily walk takes us to the end of the Bar and halfway across the bridge that connects it to the opposite shore of the bay—the bridge with concrete rails you can't see over while driving. The bridge of the double-punch. Not only does it deprive you of the privilege of seeing the geography that required bridging in the first place, it is also so smoothly continuous with the road that you can hardly tell a bridge exists. A design and engineering achievement in cancelling out the landscape.

We lean over the rail for a brief rest and watch the carp in the still, elongated pond thirty metres below, as they roil and seethe in eel-like clusters close to the surface. The carp have been roiling every day that we've stopped there to rest; a strange, grotesque and slightly unnerving sight. The liquid version of snakes in a pit.

"The kind of place you might want to throw certain politicians into. Or bridge designers," I said.

"Maybe there's one down there," she replied.

Then it's three kilometres back to the car, again at a brisk clip. For the good of our bodies. Other walkers and runners often pass us, going one way or the other, and today a fifty-ish male, skinny and muscled, loped toward and past us, bumping us with the whoompf of his slightly damp slipstream. We allowed him to jog out of earshot, which took no time at all, before we began bantering his physical attributes back and forth. Mary appreciated certain aspects of the slenderness. I saw only flesh stretched over skeleton. Neither of us felt the slightest inclination to the long-term, religious dedication required to reach his state of transcendent emaciation.

*End of the Iroquois Bar*

Just as the jogger passed, something behind my left knee went wonky. It still feels wonky, and we've decided to give these daily forays across the Bar a short break.

TONIGHT I'VE RETURNED ON MY OWN, knee or not. The car is

parked at the lay-by, on the line between the cholera stone and the blue shield, keeping a solo vigil. I've begun to feel strange about sitting alone in a parked car there anyway. It is the evening of the autumn equinox and I plan to spend it sitting by the High Level Bridge. The observance will mean overstaying the fifteen-minute allowance of parking time, thus breaking the law. Oriah knows not what she hath wrought.

For sixty years, this bridge at the centre of the landscape was called simply the High Level. In the 1980s it needed repair. Initially, City Hall planned to tear down this structure, with its four stone pylons, period lighting and decorative, open railings, and build one that would aggressively ignore its surroundings rather than ennoble them. In the tradition of the newer bridge up the road. A few unsung, local heroes campaigned strongly against the destruction, and won. A plaque commending city council was mounted to one of the pylons after the restoration, with the new, official name: Thomas B. McQuesten High Level Bridge.

At about the same time, the blue shield was erected across the road from the cholera stone, in honour of the same person, "for combining function with aesthetics in road and bridge design during his tenure as the provincial Minister of Transportation." Mr. McQuesten, lawyer, city alderman, parks board chair, and an earlier local hero of the landscape, received his public due, at last, more than half a century after the fact, and by the skin of his teeth. The shield makes no specific reference to the High Level Bridge, nor to the restoration of Burlington Heights, nor to the Royal Botanical Gardens, which were also done under his civic watch. For all his efforts in the city, and in the province, McQuesten has managed to maintain a kind of invisibility. Which, frankly, is how he wanted it.

I want to maintain invisibility too, for my sit-down equinoctial observance. Approaching the bridge, I scout for seating possibilities that will provide a view of the marsh and sunset but allow me to be out of sight of traffic passing by on York Boulevard. A short, narrow avenue of grass lies between the guardrail and the marsh slope of the Bar, which drops twenty-five metres down to the highway. A number of black willow trees grow wild on this steep embankment.

Three months ago, at the summer solstice, I stood at a gap in these willows. More of Oriah's doing. Tall grass grew on the slope at the time. The wind coming off the water was animating the grass, which swayed and swept in a random rhythm. Sometimes all that is required is to stop and watch, and the surrounding landscape will proceed to draw you in and hypnotize you. By the time I snapped out of total engrossment in the textures of the blowing grass and in the changing colours on the water, of the clouds, and began to pull myself away, I found that one of the tall stems had somehow managed to orchestrate its way into my pocket. It was stuck there. Cute. The landscape was attached to me.

A hubcap lies in the grass now, marking the place where I'd stood. To get there from the road, it had to hop the curb and travel across the sidewalk, then jump the guardrail and roll across the grass. Pretty deft for a hubcap. I am tempted to choose the spot as my seating location, but my mind is set on the pine trees growing on the round shoulder of the canal cut, where the bridge leaps across the channel.

This area north of the bridge is part of the Broman Lands,

and the small, ragged group of pines is a remnant of Matt Broman's original landscaping—he who "shared his vision of this great landscape," as the plaque on the turtle-shaped rock says. The trees do, in fact, look like landscape architecture. They look as though they were envisioned on a sheet of paper, as green accent drawn against a pale brown-grey rendering of the bridge. The result, to me, is that they partake of the 1930s aura of the bridge itself. Life is hard on this windblown shoulder, however, and despite seventy years the huddle of pines is not a tall one. Their rings are packed tight.

I come to the edge looking for a way into their huddle, and find a fishing path that plunges straight down to the canal. Soon I am among the branches and needles. It is exactly the wrong place to be. Mary had said that when we crossed the High Level the exhaust from the highway below almost overpowered her, and though I didn't notice it myself then, I do now. The pine needles act as a filter for the windblown fumes, the odour offerings to the gods of internal combustion, and exhaust hangs heavily within the branches. I am smudged with must.

So much for trying to enter and share the vision of the man who drew and planted trees. The pines are better experienced as they were conceived, that is to say visually, and from a distance. Picking the burrs off my sleeves and pant legs I climb up, re-emerge onto the grass and wander back to where the hubcap lies.

The recent rain makes it easy, almost too easy, to slide through the gap between the black willows and down the embankment slope a couple of metres. Clutching the grass, I wedge my heels into place beneath me to keep from sliding further, and plant my palms on the ground.

*Head of the Lake*

Now I feel in place: invisible from the road, with my own private view to the west, from whence cometh strength of will, or generosity of heart—I can't remember which. Sitting here, more than Oriah's Long Prayer comes to mind. My position is similar to the one we took afterward for the blessing, though on a severe slant. Hands on the ground. Breathe in, and imagine Grandmother Earth coming up through your hands, your arms and into your body.

The people who came to the ceremony on that winter solstice evening were only looking for some consolation. Some expression of mind, body and spirit that could reconcile their spiritual yearnings and needs with the world around them, both the natural world and their habited world of the city. The ceremony addressed these needs in a way that didn't seem unnatural itself. Only when we stretched out on the carpet and the music wafted and the guided dreaming began did I begin to wonder, perhaps unfairly, just how grab bag the evening's religious expression was. Because it *did* seem religious.

Later, when I tried to figure out why I wouldn't be returning to DreamStar Lodge, the reasons had more to do with my Judaeo-Christianity than with spiritual grab bags, or with the appropriation of native cultural traditions, which might also have been an issue. Shaking off more than two thousand years was no more likely for me than shaking off my own skin. It turned out that I didn't care to do the shake, either. Born and raised on the protesting side of the Catholic/Protestant equation, the whole business had become part of my internal structure. This was my personal landscape, for better or worse, and if I was to find a way into the physical and spiritual geography of my earthly dwelling place, the path would have to wend its way through the features of that inner landscape as well.

And I missed the violence. At some point during the peaceful flow of the Solstice Ceremony I realized that I am accustomed to a spirituality that puts a horrific, violent act front and centre, just above eye level, where you can't miss it. The criss-cross lines invite you to feel yourself one of the sorrowers in a great loss, to mourn your heart out, while at the same time placing you face to face with your own human complicity, where you can safely own up to your own murderous or near-murderous inclinations and acts, which may or may not be legion. It's cathartic. In the crowd that gathers each Sunday morning, mourner and murderer mingle, become indistinguishable.

Violence was part of native life and ceremony, of course, though my knowledge of it is further removed than third-hand, and suspect. I have, for instance, a vivid memory of the English actor Richard Harris hanging suspended in the air from two cords that are probably intended to mimic the stretched muscle of some poor beast. The cords have been threaded through his chest with a couple of sharp bones that prevent them from pulling out as he hangs there, swaying in pain. The scene was a re-enactment of a native initiation ceremony in the movie *A Man Called Horse*.

The portrayal of the ceremony may be wildly inaccurate, and in any case my example here is a rather extreme one, but native life was more intimate with violence in the first person, so to speak, and as a fact of human existence. It had to be: they hunted and killed their own animals for food and clothing. Denial was not an option, as it is for us. Perhaps Oriah and DreamStar Lodge conduct other ceremonies that acknowledge by what violence our lives are actually led, its inescapability and our need to respond to it. The only response I could see being encouraged at the Winter Solstice Ceremony was to the need for our own individual spiritual growth.

In the end, the evening became "merely" spiritual, if I can say that. I thought of it as water. Water you can stand in, dwell in, that you can float upon. Water to the brim, that you drink in, drink up. Clear and untainted. Water that drowns no one in a flash flood, carves no ravines, that contains no leachate or effluent, no slow breakdown of a naked doll's plastic, and no exhaust fumes that have settled on its surface from our drive to the ceremony itself. Water without blood.

The cross hanging in the front of the building I return to each Sunday morning makes more sense to me now, in a language somewhat other than the language I heard as a child sitting in the pew. The loss that stares one in the face is the loss of a single human life through slow, violent death, through the communally and politically sanctioned murder of a person who didn't do it—a person at least as innocent as the rest of us usually feel. And because the body hangs on a tree, its loss grows roots that extend downward into all the ways that the earth itself also is made to suffer.

I place myself in the company of one who gave up his own blamelessness.

THE IMAGE OF GRANDMOTHER EARTH is strong, though, and powerfully attractive, especially since my own grandmother came back so unexpectedly and wonderfully in the landscape. Grandfather Sky requires extra effort. His weather worn face of experience, wisdom and benevolence is up against the white-haired, bearded visage of a European Über-Dad: Uncle Santa's less tolerant older brother, the one with the temper, who ascended to the throne of western Christian religion long ago and is only now slowly stepping down—maybe. You don't even have to believe in him for him to be there.

The grandparents are a compelling antidote to the old guy, in part because of their implicit non-judgment. Having fulfilled their own parental responsibilities and made all the mistakes of parents, grandparents lay neither expectation nor censure on the grandchildren. They're good company. Pure pleasure is involved, the pleasure of being alive, of each other's very human being. They can see and call the child to its own true self. At the same time, accepting their advice does not diminish or compromise the child's individuality.

Seeing ancestors, forebears, within the surrounding physical world also confirms the intimate relationship between people and earth, the inseparability. The earth deserves exactly the same respect and care that the oldest living people to whom you are physically related deserve. Hurting them is quite literally hurting yourself, because you follow them. You will be born with the wounds you inflict.

My own grandparents would perform the proverbial rollover in their graves if they heard this kind of talk, mind you. As would Mary's.

THE SLEEPING GIANT has much in common with Grandmother Earth and Grandfather Sky, and the grandparents in our family photo albums wouldn't think much of him either. In the down-to-earth, non-fiction world of our parents' parents, the giant would be a "story"—and stories are not true.

The giant appears in both native and western cultures.

Where I first learned of him was in a poem called *The Sleeping Lord*, written by the Anglo-Welsh writer and painter, David Jones. The setting for the poem is Wales, one of the Welsh King Arthur stories, in which King Arthur chases the Boar who has been ravaging the landscape. The two have fought, but Arthur is able neither to kill nor capture the Boar.

In the poem, Arthur comes to embody the ravaged landscape itself and everyone who loved, or loves, the landscape—past, present and future—and everyone who fought, or fights for it. The Boar, still at large, is representative of every force that has ever done damage to the place, whether that be the invading armies of ancient Romans or the more recent coal mining companies that have eaten the hillsides. Arthur now sleeps, wounded.

> Are the slumbering valleys
>     him in slumber
>     are the still undulations
> the still limbs of him sleeping?
> Is the configuration of the land
>     the furrowed body of the lord
> are the scarred ridges
>     his dented greaves
> do the trickling gullies
>     yet drain his hog-wounds?
> Does the land wait the sleeping lord
>     or is the wasted land
> that very lord who sleeps?

Almost everything I have written in the past twenty-some years, I see now, has roots in these closing lines of the poem.

I once happened upon a postcard of a rock formation in Ontario, from an area north of Lake Superior. Superimposed on this formation was a photograph of a native Canadian lying down in a full regalia of animal skins and feathers. On the back of the card was an explanatory line about how the Ojibwa people recognized the figure of Nanabush in the form of this particular rock. Obviously, anything can be converted into kitsch. In the context of a land overrun and falling under the control of outsiders, which is as true for the North American Indians as for the Welsh, the image becomes one of a people who resisted and who lost, and who have taken on the kind of patient changelessness that you can, if you wish, read into the landscape itself.

The Sleeping Giant is what used to be called a Christ-figure. It used to be all the rage to seek out Christ-figures in works of literature. I remember, for instance, sitting in class being led by the nose through certain passages of Ernest Hemingway's *The Old Man and the Sea*. But I think it's true, and there's a connection, here, between that figure and the landscape, between the suffering human body and the body of the earth. I think that what the earth does when we come to settle upon it is give up its own blamelessness.

WHERE WAS I? Sitting on a slant, Cootes Paradise before me and a sunset beginning to unfold. Sitting on the savaged arm, beside its open wound.

The deceased bracket me. Grandparents. Civic ancestors. To the right, the cholera stone sits on the end of a point, out of sight behind trees. To the left, behind the trees on a second point, is Hamilton Cemetery. I've come to slow down my experience of the place, not quite to the extent of those buried, but as close to a stop as possible.

The water of Cootes Paradise lies flat and undisturbed, mirroring the sky, its shoreline nudged by low, darkening hills. There is a northern beauty to this expanse of water. It has the presence of a lake, though really it's no more than a large reflecting pool. The water is shallow; in many places a canoe paddle will stick in mud with each stroke.

Cootes has been virtually plant-free for years, which is why it looks so lake-like. The bulrushes and other marsh flora that once grew abundantly in the mud—leaving only small patches of open water and a clear line where the canal had been dredged through—disappeared when two intrusions altered the original environs. One intrusion was a particular fish: carp. The bottom-feeding, root-pulling, European fish was introduced to North America by a breeder in the nineteenth century, and eventually escaped his pond in New York State and spread through the Great Lakes. Upon entering Cootes Paradise, the fish ate any little plant that grew, until there were none.

An anagram of carp began affecting the marsh when the surrounding population increased in the latter half of the nineteenth century and into the twentieth, and raw sewage flowed ever more abundantly down the two main streams that fed the marsh. Spencer Creek drained the area directly to the west, above Dundas Valley, as well as the effluent of the town of Dundas, while Chedoke Creek drained the area above the escarpment, running through Chedoke Valley to the south.

Conditions are improving. A waste treatment plant and containment units now help deal with the second problem, while the latest in a series of attempts to keep out the carp and to restore the bulrushes, turtles and birds involves a dam built across the mouth of the canal on the marsh side. It's visible from where I'm sitting: an assemblage of landfill and steel, with I-beams and overhead tracks, which I am nevertheless trying to see not as a visual blight ever since a friend told me it reminded him of the canal lift bridges he's seen in Dutch paintings. It does look like those bridges, somewhat. And I'm Dutch, somewhat.

Weeks were spent driving long pilings into the bottom during its construction, because the marsh mud is unfathomably deep. A single opening in the dam traps all incoming fish in a cage, the cage is hoisted up, and the carp are hand-picked from among the other fish. The more desirable pisces are allowed into the marsh, while the carp are thrown back into the canal or dispatched to another paradise. These are sizable fish, by the way, as big as a wrestler's arm. Plans to mulch them into fertilizer ended with questions of toxicity—the bay where the fish feed is not the cleanest place. While the fish are being flung over one or the other side of the dam at this end of the marsh, small patches of plants are being rooted into the marsh muck in other spots, in an attempt to jump-start the natural process of revegetation.

The idea is to restore Paradise to the place it was when Lieutenant Thomas Cootes came to visit. The Lieutenant was stationed at the British fort on the Niagara River in the late eighteenth century and used to make the journey to Head of the Lake, on leave, for the birds. Cootes liked to station himself in a chair atop the Heights and pick off the birds as they came flying over, or so the story goes. They came in numbers: birds love a marsh, and this one also happened to be on the migratory path. Being here was *his* religious experience, and I don't mean that facetiously. The place was named for the pleasure he took in returning time and again. It was named for a relationship with the place, however skewed one may think that relationship was, rather than as a reminder of a relationship with a place in another country.

Tom Cootes thought he'd died and gone to heaven, armed. I like to think that his motives went beyond the immediate pleasure of the hunt. There were, at the time, severe food shortages on the Niagara River where he was stationed, because the influx of refugees from the United States after the Revolutionary War had overwhelmed the British capacity to feed them all. Fresh fowl would have been very welcome.

As a seagull looking for a place to land, prior to blessing Oriah, I came sweeping in over the north end of the Iroquois Bar, much like traffic on Chedoke highway below me, though several storeys higher. I hung motionless in the air over a spot on the other side of the bridge from where I'm sitting—the same spot, I realize now, where I'd always imagined Tom to be seated in a chair, rifle cradled in his lap. Dreams know no anachronism: it was a folding aluminum lawn chair with plastic webbing.

Lt. Cootes must have been back at the fort that solstice evening because his place was empty, otherwise there might have been implications to hovering in the air above him, even for a dime-a-dozen seagull. Though perhaps he would have had a sketchbook on his lap for that dream occasion, not a gun, and been drawing the view, not a bead. Lady Elizabeth Simcoe wasn't the only one who carried pencil and paper in those days. British army officers were taught the art of sketching during their military training, as a way of closely observing the landscape. There were obvious strategic reasons for this, and probably less obvious non-strategic results. Sketching is a kind of knowing. The eye, in the service of the hand, must inquire very closely of the landscape, develop a real intimacy with what is before it.

But if Tom Cootes held not a pencil but a gun, and the gun was cocked, and the bird I was that evening at the Omega Centre dropped from the sky, falling at his feet rather than lighting on his shoulder, the upshot would have been much the same since his chair is currently in the middle of four lanes of York Boulevard traffic. The criss-crossing lines are forever cancelling out someone or something. And how infinitely various are the ways of violence.

A FEW DUCKS SAIL SLOWLY across the perfection of water. They leave perfectly expanding vees in their wake; liquid elongated hills, miniature versions of the Bar, which undulate toward and into each other before melding into flat stillness. As twilight deepens, the water mirrors the sky's phenomenal, shifting subtlety of colour. Pink, white, blue and grey, all devolving into darkness. A colour show that seems to have all the time in the world. I was not aware that twilight went on for so long outside the evenings of summer vacation, or without a beach and a lake over which to perform. I should have brought a camera.

It's as much an acknowledgement of the poverty of my own response as it is an appreciation of the scene before me that my first impulse is to snap a photograph. A sunset asks to be watched, not snapped at. I could shoot my silent, visual moment, but wouldn't that be only another kind of violence against nature, against all this freely flowing time? The power of that one moment, when developed into an image on paper, might carry the quality of truth, but in front of my eyes now is a scene that is changing and developing in every one of its moments. The moments are as inseparable from each other as if they were liquid, and whatever truth is to be found must lie within their movement, their progression and accumulation, as well as in the moments themselves. To come even close to finding this truth I have to be here, over time. Or let time be over me—whatever that means. Waves rolling over the top of the Bar.

Taking a photograph could become a way of not being here, of being *not here*; of taking objective distance from the place, refusing to participate. I can't begin to imagine what participation in this event might look like, though it seemed pretty straightforward for the three first-nation drummers that evening Mary and I biked down to the new park by the bay. Landscape photography, the images that make it into books that make it onto coffee tables, can lend a sense of inadeequacy to the landscape of home. The photos of hugely dramatic locations, celebrity Grand Canyons and Niagara Falls, can lead you to think that nature, real nature, the nature and place that can feed and heal and awe, is elsewhere. Those amazing landscapes may make you wonder why you should be attached or loyal to the one you are in, the humdrum landscape of home. Which means you might not put up much resistance when next the Boar comes ravaging.

When Lady Elizabeth came and drew her sketches and painted her watercolours, she sat and watched. Just that. No shooting, of either sort. Her eye became a hand feeling its way over the landscape like the hand of a blind person over another person's features, with the same depth of sensory attention. Toward that other kind of knowing. The landscape, like the felt body, entering into the consciousness by a different route. I would learn that touch.

MIST GATHERS AND RISES from the inlets that push liquid tongues into both shorelines of the marsh as night begins to take over from evening. The low, rolling hills come to the edge to drink, protected by the escarpment at their back— the green, rock wall of summer that becomes the brown and white wall of winter. It isn't hard to imagine the mist as first cousin to the glaciers that advanced and then lay melting in the valley break of those escarpment walls. And it isn't hard to imagine the water level coming up as high as where I am sitting, on both sides of the Bar, with the occasional wave rolling over the top and catching an unwary observer from behind.

I remember one dim, defeated day when all I wanted was to be able to see the Iroquois Bar as it had been before. Before cut or fill, before habitation in loghouse or longhouse or tent, before the iceblock in the valley of the Saint Lawrence River melted and the waters of Lake Iroquois dropped thirty metres and the elongated hump of sand and gravel was exposed naked to eye and weather. Before, before, before. When the water still filled the basin on both sides, and ran around, and waved over. While the stones clattered and the dance was still taking place. The ghost of the Iroquois Bar. Please. Just once.

Mist hung in the ravines that I crossed, one after the other, as I swept toward and into town on Chedoke highway. Exiting onto the top of the Bar, I turned at the cemetery, and parked on the point that lies to my left now. Through the trees I saw Cootes Paradise entirely shrouded. Only the tops of the hills showed above the mist. Only the very top of the

Bar was visible, too. All else was water in vapour form, the ghost of water. It took a few moments before I understood these atmospheric conditions as a desire granted.

Nothing just happens, she said.

THE TWO STREAMS, Chedoke and Spencer, that had the privilege of carrying our raw sewage into Cootes Paradise were, in their previous lives, the two that flowed from the melting glacier and filled the marsh basin on this side of the Bar. Chedoke Creek barrelled through a valley from the south, travelling almost parallel to the Bar as it streamed into the basin. Spencer Creek entered from the west, down the Dundas Valley, broadsiding Chedoke directly below my present perch.

After their crash, the two streams carried on together down the length of the Bar and around its end. But here at the accident scene, where they crossed each other's paths and churned in collision, the two ate into the side of the Bar, dug a scoop out of it. The top edges of the scoop, the tips of its horseshoe-shape, are the point to my right, on which the cholera stone rests, and the point to my left, where the cemetery is. The Bar is narrowest here because of the scoop. That's why the canal was cut through at this location, and why it became the position for the second line of defense in the War of 1812.

*What are your sources?* Mary asks, when my geo-sleuthing presents her with another find. She's a stickler.

A few books, some maps, I tell her. Looking.

When a landscape begins to inveigle itself into your consciousness, you assume it's you who's the initiator, coming and going, posing questions, nosing for answers. Later, as various pieces of its story have gathered and fallen into place, it can begin to seem as though the place itself has been tipping its hand, playing prompter. Responding. The line that divides the two of you begins to waver.

I used to wonder where all the fill was dumped when the canal was cut through the Bar in 1853. In an era of hand-shovels, buckets, carts, mules and horses, they wouldn't have wanted to carry it far. The perfect spot, I thought, would have been in the deepest section of the scoop that the glacial streams created, just below the present cemetery. It was close by, but out of the way. I'm fairly certain about the water-churning origins of the scoop itself, without having to prove it, but this time documentation was forthcoming. Among the old maps in the library I came across one drawn in 1859. Over that particular area was written: *This Portion is covered with sand taken from the Canal.*

I had done no more than come sit on the edge and let my eyes settle. I tried to touch the line where the surface we live upon touches the surface we cannot. Something happened here. The questions asked themselves. Where did the sand and gravel go? Why is the Bar narrower? Slowly the ice melted and the water was freed all over again, and a land feature that was so solid and stationary when I crossed every day began to move and sway like a floating dock, and I rose and fell with the motion of the memory contained in these shapes crafted by natural and human event.

IT SOUNDS LIKE WATER, the noise coming from all those lines and lanes of traffic, above and below. The sound comes in waves, heavy and light, though without the consistency or regular rhythm of waves of water. Not a lake, then; not the pounded beach of glacial Iroquois or Algonquin; not even Ontario. A waterfall? Too heavy for Albion Falls. Niagara Falls then? But lacking the changeless, liquid wall of sound—for there *are* waves. So much for trying to naturalize the sound of highway traffic. If it were even desirable.

Did Oriah instruct us to close our eyes when we imagined the energy of Grandmother Earth entering our hands through the layers of concrete on which we sat cross-legged? She did: I remember looking into her closed eyes. If you close your eyes here on this slanted embankment, the aural override of cars and trucks fades briefly into the background, but the irregularity of the waves, the accelerations, the shifting gears of eighteen-wheelers, soon breaks through any meditative concentration and brings you back to where you are.

Here on the savaged arm of the sleeping giant you have to keep both eyes open. You never know when the Boar will come blasting through Matt Broman's pine trees with a chainsaw, or churning through the sand-and-gravel bar with backhoes and another six-lanes of paved desecration. The theme recurs, in earth, water and now in the air: watch, wait. To think that I started the Bar vigils at the lay-by as a lark.

Is air also a part of the landscape? The part that carries sound, that we cannot see, but through which we see, hear and smell? And which we breathe, if we can. Does merely breathing make us a part of the landscape? I know that closing your eyes and trying to remain totally conscious of your breathing, among other benefits, *places* you.

When does our breath become the sky, Daddy?

I'm all over the place now. The traffic's starting to get to me. Once, while sitting in the Sunday meeting place, daydreaming during the Long Prayer, it occurred to me that if I had to locate myself, if there were one place where I could imagine myself naturally falling to earth, it would be mid-Atlantic.

Somewhere on the sea-path between the Netherlands and Canada. This was not a political statement. It had to do with a sense of physical uncertainty and unrootedness that I imagine is part of being an immigrant's child. Nothing solid underfoot. When I first saw how native Canadians danced— the step-jumping shuffle, up and down, the drum sounding both foot and heart steps—I was shot through with envy in the recognition of what I didn't have.

If I had to locate myself now ... but it's ridiculous: this spot is not serene. On the other hand, you don't necessarily choose these places. They call, and you come. Or you don't come. There's where the choice lies.

It isn't easy to be here. It wasn't easy to get here and it isn't easy to stay. During the day it's even more difficult. The sound of traffic from six lanes below and four lanes above can become as overpowering as the odour-offering of exhaust fumes wafting through the rails of the High Level Bridge, especially in the area above the churned-out scoop, which collects and amplifies the din. There, even I will consider breaking into a run, for the sound, in its unrelenting urgency, begins to feel like a form of aural torture, and it's no stretch to think it could push a person into madness.

THE STILL AND MOVING CENTRE. Still and not still. Where the lines cross, natural and human, past and present. The meeting, middle of things. Water currents meeting air currents meeting human currents. Roadway and railway rolling north-south, criss-cross with fish swimming east-west (excepting carp). Cormorants paddling the air between the high stone pylons that stand on either end of the bridge as though the birds were following a marked route, riding winds that funnel through the narrow opening cut into the Bar. While hawks ride the thermals that rise from the Bar.

On the marsh side, one glacial meltwater stream is broadsided by another, and they thrash it out. Above their meeting lie settlers and citizens, immigrants and soldiers.

And nothing just happens.

On the bay side, lake current meets current coming around the end of the Bar, and their head-on collision becomes a whirlpool that takes and shapes the sand and gravel into another point of land, a smaller peninsula, a miniature bar fashioned out of the Bar's side. As the currents eddy in the confinement of this tip end of the Great Lake, they actually create two such long fingers of land, the second taken from the side of the opposite shoreline, Carroll's Point—where the four of us, plus children, found ourselves so pleased with this place, the improbable silence, the lapping waters, the patrolling swans, that we wished we'd brought supplies so we could do the Simcoe dinner-thing.

It wasn't easy to get to Carroll's Point, either. Is there something in the nature of this place where the lines converge that makes it both difficult to get to and a challenge to stay? That pushes as it pulls?

Hamilton itself is a bit of an anomaly in that, geographically, it's avoidable. The city sits in the middle of a U-shaped string of cities and towns, sometimes called the Golden Horseshoe, which has grown around the western end of Lake Ontario. The bulk of highway traffic runs along the lake shoreline and rounds the end of the lake by crossing the sandbar that lies at the mouth of the bay, cutting-off and entirely bypassing Hamilton while providing a terrific view of the industry concentrated at that end of the bay.

From the east, you enter the city through a narrow corridor between escarpment and lake, from the west by winding through a valley that is the one break in the escarpment's wall, from the south by climbing down that wall, and from the north only by crossing a narrow causeway of the Iroquois Bar. Perhaps "avoidable" is inaccurate. It might be better to say that you have to want to get here.

It becomes more interesting all the time. The city embodies the same contradictions that centre around this piece of geography called the Iroquois Bar.

Some of us do want to get here. Once, returning from a trip to Chicago, a journey of seven hundred kilometres, *through country best described as unrelieved* (a phrase from a poem by Richard Wilbur), Mary and I realized as we neared home that the most interesting portion of the entire trip, geographically, was its last five minutes. From the moment we broke over the top edge of the escarpment overlooking the Dundas Valley, we relaxed. And took it all in. Driving down, the rock wall grew higher on our right side as the view spread out wider before us of valley and city, marsh and bay, the escarpment wall of the opposite side of the valley, the trees, the city apartment towers, office towers, with the stone pylons of the Thomas B. McQuesten High Level Bridge in the very middle, and a lake beyond.

Descending into, entering this landscape, we eventually joined the same Chedoke spillway that glacial torrents once swept down, that swept us up the off-ramp and deposited us at our front door, the keys rattling in our hands.

I don't know if nature heals, but I think that it can absorb our hurts. Perhaps a landscape that has itself been most pained by its relationship to us is best able to take in our pain.

But right now I'm sitting on a steep slant, and it's gotten dark and my knee is beginning to act up. It occurs to me that in our exercise walks, Mary and I were just another part of the traffic flow, using the Bar as a transportation corridor. I had meant to treat the place differently. My invisible constant companion, the nagging, ancient Protester, tells me I deserve my wonky knee.

Clinging to the long grass, I haul myself to the top and pick up the hubcap that's still lying there. A friend once gave me a few sheets photocopied from a dictionary of symbols. The circle: traditional symbol for completeness, perfection, oneness. A car has four of them. Circles within circles: hubcaps within wheels. Cars must represent the epitome of completeness. There's a circle for each of the four cardinal directions a car can travel, the four directions of Oriah's prayers. Inside, the driver holds a fifth wheel, the one that provides control over destination, that gives the illusion of control over destiny. Meanwhile, the body of a car is defined by a box, its wheels set in corners of a square. The square a symbol of incompleteness, an inner unity not achieved. Our primary mode of land transportation seems to be travelling in two directions at once, symbolically speaking.

A woman is walking on the opposite side of the road, in the same direction I need to walk to get to the car. Someone's granddaughter. By the way she looks at me over her shoulder and quickly keeps moving, I realize that she must have seen me just at the moment when I emerged, in the street-lit dark, from my hiding place down the slope of the embankment. That should make me suspicious enough for any passerby. But I understand now that I am just another one of the men who stop and hang out at various locations here along Burlington

Heights. You see them stopping their cars at the same lay-by where I stop for my vigils. I count their cars. They straighten out their jackets as they look one way or the other, deciding which direction to walk. They stroll around the cholera stone, by the old sunken garden with its empty reflecting pool, or up the steps to McQuesten's shield. They observe and have even followed my scouting around. They are why I am reluctant to sit in my parked car anymore. Whether or not they come for the same reasons as I, to this woman I am one of them.

She turns and crosses the road to my side, walking directly toward me, confronting head-on whatever dark possibilites might be preying on her mind, determined not to make eye contact, and equally determined not to have me decide where she will or will not walk. Our paths meet and cross. Soon she'll be over the bridge, will pass by Tom Coote's lawn chair and enter the area above the scoop where the highway sound will be loudest, and where it first occured to me that this whole venture into one particular place, one piece of geography, has everything to do with relation. A series of interconnected, overlapping relationships that reach further and further out. Relation and reciprocity.

I place the hubcap in the trunk of the car and begin driving home, overtaking and passing the woman as she jogs the sidewalk between the wrought iron fence of the cemetery and the line of pine trees. Then I'm slipping, slinking, down the side of the Bar, home.

# Selective Memory

THEY ACCRETE. COLLECT. Some motion of wind or water carries and deposits each of these objects to where it arrests the eye of the walker. A sewer grate not quite level with the road surface delivers the jolt to a passing vehicle that sets a loose part free. The reflected clouds and sky disappear as a pane of glass slides down into the car door and an invisible hand jettisons overboard some small piece from the world inside.

Garbage.

Most of the pieces and parts are as mass-produced as the stones that make up the glacial sand-and-gravel bar they land upon. A small, white plastic snowman from the sidewalk in front of the cholera stone. An amber lens from the tail light of a truck, lying on the off-ramp. A vinyl-wrapped piece of cardboard designed to be wedged into the gap between the hood and fender of a car: FUNERAL. The left leg of a baby doll. A pop can, brand-named Master Choice, flattened by a car. A penny, flattened by a train.

My younger daughter, who is a frequent companion on these rambling explorations of the Bar, calls it "valuable junk."

A small, green, plastic Iroquois warrior, poised for attack, brandishing tomahawk and knife.

An empty cardboard take-out coffee cup.

A hubcap.

She draws a line at the used coffee cup, though the cup is thoroughly rinsed. Together the pieces of junk set up a silent conversation on a shelf that has been emptied of its books. We are no longer going by the book, but by the place.

The display requires a verbal gloss for each item, one that explains the circumstances under which it was found: the rusted nut and eight-inch-long bolt picked up beside railway tracks, during a walk with children, on which we saw swans; the glass insulator that bears a resemblance to the Buddha, unscrewed from a telephone pole that lay snapped in half at ground level like a toothpick, from the same walk.

It's reminiscent of the display cases in old museums. Thomas Barnett's Niagara Falls Museum, founded 1827, still has the cases, as did Dundurn Castle in the years following its purchase by the city: the long, glass counters in which an assortment of family treasures, long-held collectibles and odds and ends dug up in the backyard, is laid out. The stuff of someone's attic. Sometimes the only connection between the objects, between the broken china and the brass button, is the person who found them. They are intimate, and idiosyncratic. They might have nothing to do, geographically or historically, with the place where they are displayed: Sitting Bull's mocassin lies in the museum in Niagara Falls. Or the intersection of the object and the place it has landed grows its own history. Leo the Lion, a favourite at the Dundurn Park Zoo, was mounted and put on display in Dundurn Castle after his demise. When the museum closed in the 1940s, many of the museum pieces were auctioned off or otherwise disposed of. Leo was last seen leaving in the back of a pickup.

These lost and thrown-away bits of detritus on the shelf at home represent the next layer of sedimentation, a kind of urban moraine. Picking one up off the ground is an act of surface archaeology. I readily concede that separately and together they have less meaning than the eighteenth-century brass military buttons and shards of crockery that have been found in the soil at the bottom of the ravine where the Beasleys lived. But the collection reminds me of the beauty of finding things, when the object shines from the ground where it lies. Where the object's importance is partly event. When the object shines from the ground where it lies. I showed the shelf to the friend who owned the dictionary of symbols, and she returned several days later with another book, pointing to a line that spoke about the sacramental power of objects that are given and received in the right spirit.

One may always question whether one's spirit is right, but may I think of these objects picked off the ground, this garbage, as given?

MERCER'S GLEN

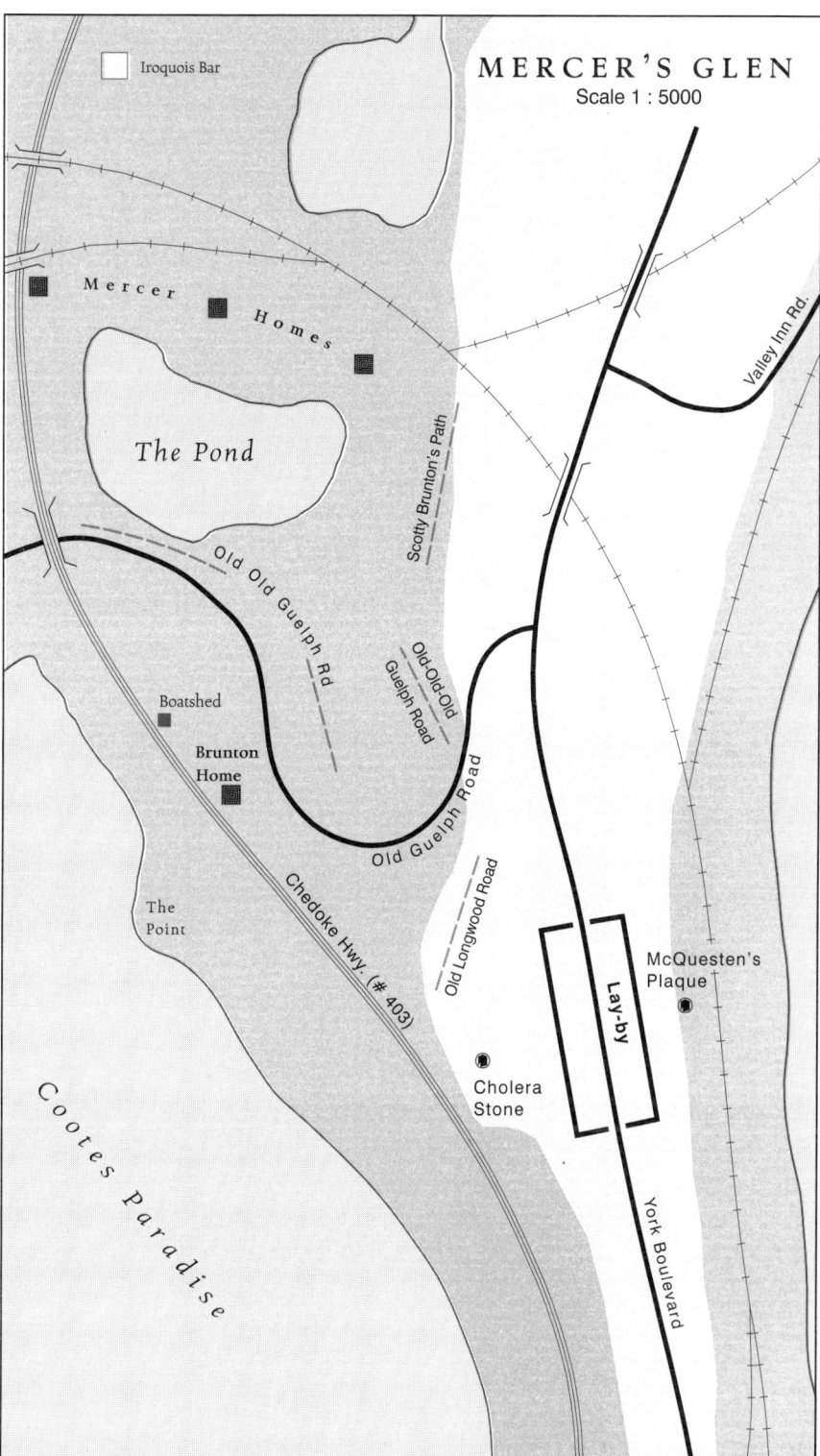

# Selective Memory: *Always Fresh*

A FIVE-INCH-HIGH, gently tapered cylinder of poly-lined paper, stopped at its narrow end. Dark brown, with a large yellow and brown logo printed on it. The cup measures two inches across at its bottom, and three at its top. The open top is covered by a plastic lid, which has a one-inch wide flap extending from the lip to the centre. Crayoned in blue on the lid is the letter "C." Cream in his coffee.

Of the nine hundred and twenty million ounces of takeout coffee poured from all the coffee pots in all the Tim Hortons Donut shops across the nation that year, fourteen ounces were poured into this cup.

"I guess I can give you that information. You're obviously not going to use it against us."

The company representative on the phone had been reluctant to give out any company facts until she became convinced that her caller was not trading in industry secrets.

*Always Fresh. Please Do Not Litter.*

The cup is biodegradable, she said. Its lid is not. The lid, however, may be recycled, if facilities exist in your area.

The cup was removed from the crotch of a small tree growing near the base of the railway embankment at a spot called Mercer's Glen, on the marsh side of the Iroquois Bar. I fought my way across the Glen through the bulrushes and spent half an hour trying to locate the tree, which seemed to have vanished from the day before, in order to retrieve it. The cup was wedged into place between trunk and branch. The fraction of an ounce of coffee left in the cup had been sufficient to kill the cigarette butt that lay saturated at the bottom. Export A, Plain. I tipped the butt out and rinsed the cup, thoroughly, before placing it on the shelf with the other valuable junk, where it enters the silent conversation.

# Mercer's Glen

IMMEDIATELY BEYOND the lay-by, past the imaginary line that's stretched across York Boulevard between Thomas B. McQuesten's shield and the cholera stone, is the option of a left-hand turn. Old Guelph Road describes a leisurely hairpin as it descends from the Heights—left, right, then left again—presenting as it turns a view of Cootes Paradise, then Chedoke highway, and then the railway landfill dam that blocked the original outlet around the end of the Bar, before slipping through a tunnel under the highway and climbing the north shore of the marsh.

For years, a wooden post stood mounted on a low embankment where the road reaches its lowest point at the water level of the former channel around the end of the Iroquois Bar. The embankment lies between and parallel to the road and the much higher railway embankment. Between those two embankments, most years, is a pond. A board was attached to the post, and routed into it were the words "Mercer's Glen." The letters were all capitals, painted yellow against the board's dark brown. Simple and declarative, and typical of the signs that the Royal Botanical Gardens used at the time to mark the trails and features of its landholdings, of which the Glen was, and is, one. The sign often required replacing, and when it last went missing no one bothered.

By the time my accumulated daily drives down through that area were totalling four thousand—twice a day, more or less, for ten years—and finally beginning to make me curious, the sign had been gone for several years already. But when I wanted to know more about the place, I did what I've come to learn is the simplest and most direct route into the past here, and looked up the name in the phone book.

A woman answered the first call. She said, "Oh, you want to talk to my uncle." She was the niece of someone who had spent his childhood playing at Mercer's Glen. On the second call I was talking to George Mercer.

Perhaps I shouldn't be surprised that people stay living here, Beasley-like, for generations, but to this son of immigrant parents who moved twice, back and forth across the country of their choice, *after* their big move across the ocean, it comes as a revelation. You don't have to be part of an oceanic or continental migration, either, to get the distinct impression that in our culture mobility is considered a virtue: you should be able to pick up and leave wherever you are, whenever you wish or are called upon to do so. You *must* be able to: it's a requirement that almost defines what we think of as a person's individuality. You'd be considered somehow deficient without it. It goes even further: you must *want* to move. We're like the cars we drive: absolutely independent entities, a contradiction in terms when parked. To wish or choose to stay where you are, to maintain your geographical location, is almost an act of subversion, tantamount to burning your identity card. It's as though the longer you live in a place the more you are forced to feel that you do not belong. You become, strangely, a resident alien.

As children, George and his younger brother, Al, often walked from their neighbourhood in the city to visit their grandmother, who lived at the Glen, and to fish. This was in the 1950s. I had heard Granny Mercer's name before, from others who used to frequent the areas in and around Cootes Paradise as kids, and who also used to pay her visits at the small pond between Old Guelph Road and the railway embankment, but somehow I had never connected her name with the vanished signpost. Both George and Al live on the other side of the city now. When I talked to them, neither had been back to the Glen in the thirty-five years since Granny died, when her house was expropriated and razed, and Chedoke highway came through. They agreed to meet me there.

I ARRIVED EARLY. Four thousand times passing through, and this was the first time I stopped at Mercer's Glen. I'd never thought to stop. To be perfectly honest there's not much attraction, and really no place to pull over. I mounted the curb and parked on the shoulder, then walked up the embankment beside the road to the spot where the signpost had stood. I was surprised, yet again, at just how much larger a place is, seen in person, than it seems from a passing vehicle. Cars diminish a landscape.

The stomping ground of George and Al Mercer's youth lies enclosed within four walls: the Iroquois Bar; the landfilled, giant's finger of the first railway; the raised bed of the six-lane, Chedoke highway; and Old Guelph Road itself. Only the first two existed when the boys came to visit. Granny's home sat at the base of the railway's high, steep slope, with a view that opened to the southwest over Cootes Paradise, a view blocked now by the highway. I stood at centre field, at the bottom of an amphitheatre enclosed by one natural and three man-made embankments, with Old Guelph Road descending into the middle of it like a processional ramp from the nosebleed section. Mercer's Bowl would be a more descriptive name now.

Let the games begin.

I was beginning to wonder if I'd gotten my wires crossed about our meeting time when a large van drove slowly down Old Guelph Road, flicked on its signal light and turned into the driveway of the Garden's composting area, followed by a pickup truck. George and his wife Jean emerged from the first vehicle, and Al and his wife Val from the second. Introductions were made.

"Why are you so interested in this place, anyway?" Al asked. He seemed suspicious. Jean and Val opted to stay in the vehicles, while the three of us stepped over the chain that barred the drive.

A large black willow tree grew beside the driveway, just inside the compost area, and we stood under it as the brothers tried to take their bearings. Memories began to spark almost immediately. George said the driveway was in the same location, exactly, as the old turnoff to Granny's house. Both soon became convinced that this black willow was the same tree that stood at the corner where Old Guelph Road and the turnoff to Granny's intersected, when they were young. I wondered if a tree large enough to be remembered thirty-five years later would still be standing. Black willows grow quickly but are not especially long-lived. I also knew a little about the former configuration of the roads—they've been re-configured more than once—and questioned whether the Old Guelph Road of their time would have run by this spot.

We looked down and in the direction from which, by their reckoning, Old Guelph Road would have come, and lo, before us lay a clear, ten-metre stretch of pavement. It ran parallel to the present Old Guelph Road before slipping under the embankment of the newer road as the newer one curved and climbed over it, like one leg crossing another. A five-metre-high mound of dead Christmas trees stood stacked on the old pavement there.

A section of the *old* Old Guelph Road. George and Al were right. If the tree beside us wasn't their willow, it could well be that willow's offspring. The old road lined up, too, both in its curve and grade, with the embankment where the Mercer's Glen post had stood, making that lower embankment a likely portion of the road as well—the portion that crossed the water between the Bar and the marsh's north shore, and that separated Cootes Paradise from the Glen. And so another couple of remnants could be added to my list of paths and roads, the traces of former ways of getting around that lay scattered over the Bar like the scars of old wounds.

The three of us turned and started walking toward the Bar. The pond lay to our left, but as far as we could tell it was completely dry, covered in bulrushes. The laneway to Granny's soon was buried under a mattress of organic waste, the Garden's thirty-year collection of clippings and prunings. As we reached the base of the Bar, we found ourselves having to negotiate our way down the mattress's frayed edge; a jagged, hazardous, two-and-a-half-metre journey through a madness of branches as thick and stiff as broken ladder rungs. At the bottom, we then worked our way through a living version of this same thicket. This was not the lane to Granny's as George or Al remembered it.

The laneway had been no wider than a single vehicle. It had skirted between the Bar's agglomeration of small stones on one side and the pond on the other. Each year, a City of Hamilton works truck would stop at the spot where the lane squeezed between rock and water, and two city workers would emerge to install a gate and block access. The city boundary ran there, and the gate had something to do with the city maintaining a claim over the right-of-way, which crossed into the neighbouring township at that point, while not accepting responsibility for its maintenance. No one paid much attention, however, and after a few weeks the gate would mysteriously disappear, again.

It was still missing, along with the laneway it had attempted to block. Also absent was the arm of rock that once stuck out from the side of the Bar, scraping cars and removing the occasional sideview mirror, and a second, bigger rock: a solid rump of cemented Iroquois Bar stones that lane-users called Ass Rock. After their initial success at the black willow, George and Al were coming up short on physical landmarks. We fought bush and burr, and skirted the quaking aspen trees that stood sentry around three sides of the Glen and that reached up as high as the tops of the railway embankment and the Bar itself. The aspens rattled their thousand green details over our heads. These were the new landmarks: none grew in the Mercers' time.

We looked for the paths that led down the Bar, that George and Al had taken on the days they walked to the Glen from the city. They'd been told to avoid the steeper path, because rattlesnakes were said to hide in the cool, cave-like, undercut sides of the Bar where it passed. Another path had followed the side of the Bar from the top of the railway embankment, coming out at the city gate. It served as a commuter line for Granny's neighbour, Graham Brunton.

The Brunton family—Graham, his wife Margaret, their daughter Margaret and son Colin—lived on the opposite side of the old Old Guelph Road, on a large strip of land between the road and the marsh shore. Graham had climbed up the path to work as the first caretaker of the Rock Garden, above Mercer's Glen, on top of the Bar. The Rock Garden was one of the projects that reclaimed the landscape of and around the Iroquois Bar from the 1920s through the 40s. An abandoned quarry used a decade earlier to supply gravel for the first Hamilton-Toronto Highway became transformed into a floral bowl. For a long time the Rock Garden was the Royal Botanical Gardens' main claim to fame, and an identifying tourist attraction for the city. We knew about it way out west in Edmonton, where I was a child. Scotty Brunton had been climbing the path to reach and tend its flowers and trees since before opening day. His nickname came courtesy of the accent in his immigrant voice.

But George and Al had no luck finding either Scotty's or the rattlesnakes' path.

Where the old laneway met the railway embankment it made a ninety-degree left turn, and at the turn there had been a spring. A ladle hung beside the spring, from which you could drink the "coldest, clearest, sweetest-tasting water" that George ever remembered drinking. When he and I talked initially on the phone, this was one of the first memories that came to mind for him, and he repeated it as we stood at the spot. You can't escape the sense of tremendous, hidden, personal significance in the stories that spring to people's minds and mouths when the place where a particular past is stored is touched, and the clearest, sweetest-tasting memory bubbles up.

No spring now, of course.

We began walking along the base of the railway embankment. The first of the three small Mercer homes stood close to the spring, and all three drew their water from it. Three of George and Al's uncles shared the first and last house, while Granny occupied the one in the middle. The structures were homes because people lived in them, but they were constructed in a time before the building code was written, and more than a few current bylaws were actively contravened. The two young grandchildren had been warned never to go into Granny Mercer's bedroom because the floor might be under water.

In the eyes of the people then beginning to move into the brick houses being built on the other side of Cootes Paradise during the period between the two world wars, or who travelled to and from their growing suburban neighbourhoods via the new two-lane road that ran along the marsh shoreline and climbed to the top of the Bar just above where the Mercers lived, the Mercer homes were indistinguishable from the boathouses that stood around the Desjardins Canal. They looked rustic, or ramshackle, depending on your point of view. A step or so above simple shelter, these supremely humble dwellings were not uncommon in urban areas at the time. Mercer's Glen was fortunately tucked into a corner of the landscape, mercifully hidden behind trees, out of the refined driver's eyesight. The rack of moose antlers that hung above Granny's front door faced the railway embankment, greeting only residents and guests.

We reached the spot where her house had stood. Or so they thought. In trying to pinpoint the exact location, George and Al were receiving very little help from the physical surroundings. The steep slopes of the Bar and the railway embankment, bare and brown in their youth, now lay covered in bush which obscured whatever landmarks might have remained. The hollow their grandfather had dug into the side of the railway embankment as a turnaround for vehicles, was nowhere to be found. The brothers were guessing, trying to place their adult bodies, thirty-five years later, into the feel of the landscape of their childhood. They may as well have been going by the stars.

Yet another path led straight down from the railway tracks and came out beside their grandfather's turnaround hollow. George and Al occasionally used that path if they walked to the Glen along the tracks. The same path had been followed twenty years earlier during the Depression by some of the unemployed men who followed their noses to Granny's door. The men travelled the railway and stayed at the outdoor hobo hotel at the top of the embankment. The story at the hotel went that Granny Mercer kept a pot of soup on the stove.

She observed the men climb carefully down the steep slope where she sat reading detective stories from a magazine at her kitchen table.

"You hungry?" she asked when they knocked. She offered a filled bowl, a spoon and a place to sit, and she watched as they ate. As the last spoonful travelled to their mouths, she'd reclaim bowl and cutlery.

"You've had your meal, now go." Granny was known as accommodating, generous, and no-nonsense.

The path that led to the free meal wound between rocks on its way down to Granny's—an organized display of rocks. The rocks were not a natural feature of the railway embankment, any more than the embankment itself was a natural feature of the glaciated landscape. Similarly sized, round, and painted white, the rocks were arranged in letters across the slope,

MERCERS GLEN

with no apostrophe to indicate possession. Possession was not in question here.

George and Al's grandfather had laid the stones in letters large enough to be read from the opposite side of Cootes Paradise, by those city and suburban motorists travelling to and from their new homes. Their grandfather, for whom George was named, laid familial claim to a landscape to which the railway he lived beside and below had laid industrial claim half a century earlier. George Sr. died before the brothers were born, but for George and Al the Glen was a true inheritance, the best kind of gift, a place in the country the city kids could call their own.

EMILY AND GEORGE MERCER SR. raised nine children at the Glen, so each of the three dwellings was needed and used. George Sr. had worked on the first bridge between the end of the Bar and the north shoreline during the construction of the Hamilton-Toronto Highway, in 1917. Injured on the job, he wasn't able to work again afterward. He built the first and third of the three houses at the Glen himself, but the one in the middle, that eventually became known as Granny's, was already standing when the young couple first arrived. It wasn't standing at the base of the railway embankment, however.

We now enter a landscape where some of the painted rocks on the slope of the story were placed by George and Al, and others by their uncle, John, while some come from my own rockhounding ways.

A common feature at the perimeter of an urban centre toward the end of the nineteenth century was the toll house and gate. Private companies often owned the roadways, and hired and housed toll keepers to collect money, for maintenance and profit, from travellers entering the city. Many travellers, especially farmers carting crops and produce to market, were of the opinion that profit came before maintenance for the companies, because roads were in bad repair and tolls high. Complaints grew louder, a public roads movement started, and eventually farmers took matters into their own hands by refusing to pay tolls, destroying gates and even torching the houses where the toll keepers lived. The private toll road system collapsed shortly before the end of the century, around the same time that the first automobile made its appearance.

John Mercer, Emily and George's youngest son, isn't so certain that his childhood home originally served as a toll house. He is the last surviving of the nine children; Uncle Johnny to his nephews George and Al, who introduced us. In the family story, Johnny's father bought the house from the city, which had taken it over from the private company. The agreement stipulated that the house be moved. As Johnny remembered it, the house was floated across water from the other side of Cootes Paradise. In a cardboard box in his nephew George's closet, however, among other papers, is a receipt for fifty dollars that places the purchased house on the north side of the marsh, beside the road to Guelph.

The receipt gave one clue to the home's original site. There were more clues. Abandoned homesites of the time often left a small depression in the ground once the basement-less building itself had decayed or was removed, and lilac bushes often sprang up around the depression. Johnny recalled such a low area surrounded by lilacs, as did Margaret Brunton, a former playmate of his. Both grown children placed the shallow, hidden bowl beside the laneway to Granny's, at about the spot where George and Al and I had begun our walk, by the black willow. The willows grow more or less where grew the lilacs. More, rather than less. In this service area of earth flattened hard by vehicles, of mounds of organic waste and piles of soil, the familial clump of black willow has somehow remained an island that the vehicles all go around. What I consider to be the original location of the Mercer home has managed to linger into the present.

What was a toll house doing beside the laneway to Granny's? Why was it not beside the old Old Guelph Road?

On my daily drives up the lazy switchback climb of the present Old Guelph Road, I'd begun to notice a short, perfectly graded stretch of land that lay against the side of the Bar. Entirely obscured by overgrowth during the summer months, it emerged very distinctly into view after a light snowfall, when the contours of the landscape are more clearly revealed. I wondered, *road remnant*? The grade lined up perfectly with the old laneway to Granny's, which it met at the clump of black willow.

Johnny Mercer was aware of the grade and said that it had

been well used when he was young. Cars turned off old Old Guelph Road onto Granny's laneway, but where her laneway bore left to squeeze between Bar and pond, the cars forked right, up the grade, parked, and shut off their headlights. Lover's Lane. The lane had been a former road, he said.

A nineteenth-century map showing an earlier configuration of roadways confirmed the short, graded piece of earth as a remnant of the generation of roadways prior to the one George and Al and I had discovered. It was a stretch of the *old*-old-Old Guelph Road, as close to the original route taken by settlers and soldiers dismounting the Bar as one is likely to get. Simcoe's escape route off the Bar. The road in daily use when toll houses were active at the town lines, in this case the same town line that a city works truck enforces annually with a gate barring the way to Granny's, years later. The Mercer home had been floated across water, but the water was the pond at Mercer's Glen rather than Cootes Paradise. The house sailed out of the City of Hamilton and into the Town of Dundas, next door.

This account comes with a full apology to Johnny Mercer, whose conviction about the original location of his family home I don't enjoy disputing.

By now, I'd been talking to two generations about one landscape over a period of time that spanned three generations, and was having trouble keeping order in my mind. Though grateful to have a manageable section of landscape on which to focus, I found that even in such a small area the landscape had a kind of fluidity, a lapping and overlapping of time and place that it shared with the three human generations, where brothers were so spread apart in age they could be father and son, and uncles were young enough to be brothers to their nephews. Johnny admitted that he was a late baby to Emily and George. His oldest brother Alfie had already left home when he was born at the beginning of the Depression. Alfie was George and Al's father. The distance in years between Johnny and these nephews was only slightly greater than that between Johnny and Alfie.

Alfie drove truck. The Mercers' laneway ended just past the last house, which sat almost on the marsh shoreline, at the mouth of one of the shoreline ravines. The bottomlessness of the marsh has played a big part in the marsh's story over the past two hundred years. In one chapter of that story, Alfie would drive to the end of the laneway with a load of marble tile scraps from his work, and dump the scraps into the water. No matter how much marble he dumped, Johnny said, the loads always sank completely and forever out of sight.

"There's some good marble down there. And bicycles. Old car parts. You name it."

Another kind of dumping took place across the pond. Sardo's, a fruit and vegetable market in the city, unloaded spoiled produce over the embankment of old Old Guelph Road. Johnny's father occasionally retrieved edible food there for his family. At least, that's how Margaret Brunton, Johnny's former playmate, remembered it. She allowed, however, that she may have gotten the story from her mother, a woman more finely attuned to the not-so-subtle differences between the families—between the employed, such as her husband Graham, and the under- or unemployed, such as George Mercer.

"We were poor," Johnny admitted, "dirt poor. But lots of people were poor then. We never went hungry."

He said that at the time there was no shame in living where

and how they did, because many others lived in conditions no better than the Mercers'. People such as the boathouse dwellers in the community around the canal. Only in the years following World War II, Johnny said, did living on next to nothing, with next to nothing, become socially unacceptable. He understood, then, that he couldn't take a girl home anymore, and moved into the city, where he worked. The change in norms had no effect on Granny Mercer, however. She lived at the Glen until her death on Christmas Eve, 1958. Three of her sons continued living there until the living there ended completely for everyone, including the Bruntons, three years later.

GRAHAM AND MARGARET BRUNTON raised their children, Margaret and Colin, in a two-and-a-half storey brick house built on the same pattern as the houses then being constructed in the new suburb on the other side of Cootes Paradise. The house stood on a couple of acres of flat land between the marsh itself and the old Old Guelph Road, where the road ran along the base of the Bar toward the canal. Where their property ended, the boathouse community began. The Bruntons' house was owned by the Royal Botanical Gardens, and came with Scotty's job at the Rock Garden. In addition to the house and garage, the property included a small boatshed, enough acreage for a vegetable garden and a larger plot on which Scotty cultivated the varieties of lilac that became the original Lilac Dell of the Gardens.

The property also included a point of land that projected into the marsh. The point was well-known. On it stood a large willow tree with a rope hanging from a branch that kids used for swinging into the water. Not far from shore, the bottom of the marsh suddenly dropped. All the kids were aware of the drop, and knew the consequences if you swung too far out and landed above it without being able to swim back. Most of them could not swim.

The drop-off was intriguing to me. Before the railway's landfill dam blocked its passage, the Desjardins canal had come past the Bruntons' point on its way around the end of the Iroquois Bar. I wondered aloud to Johnny one day if the two—the drop-off and the canal—might be connected. He was familiar with the old canal route, and said that when he was a child two rows of posts still poked through the water of their pond. The two parallel rows defined the path of the old channel, which had been dredged. The posts shored up its sides. Hardly anything remains today of the Desjardins canal except for its cut through the Iroquois Bar, but two rows of similar posts will occasionally, at low water, during the winter, still protrude through surface level and define the path of the newer channel approaching the cut. They're visible from the High Level Bridge, the only evidence on Cootes Paradise that the marsh once was a water highway.

Johnny's posts ran from Cootes through the Glen. They leaned one way or another, were fallen over or rotted, or were missing and broke the standing line. The twin lines aimed at the middle house, where he lived, placing it directly in the pathway of the boats and barges of the previous century. He and his friends paddled to the posts bearing matches, and built small fires in the rotted, hollowed centres.

The railway created Mercer's Glen, which is really nothing more than a cul-de-sac. When the railway first came through in the 1850s, it wasn't solely a blatant disregard for the landscape that dictated a landfill dam be built from the north shore of the marsh to the Iroquois Bar. A bridge had been planned. In trying to set footings for the bridge piers it was discovered that the marsh bottom wasn't solid enough to take the weight. In fact, no bottom could be found. Eventually, the bridge idea was abandoned, and carts, shovels, wheelbarrows and mules were called in, and load after load of fill was tipped into the marsh, where it all sank forever out of sight like the bicycles and car parts and Alfie's loads of scrap marble. But the landfill wouldn't even rise to water level. It was as though they were dumping into the abyss.

A local farmer received the credit for suggesting tree stumps as a solution. A ready supply existed, since all over the countryside farmers were chopping trees and pulling up stumps as they cleared land for planting. With their hacked roots still attached, the stumps sank only so far before hanging suspended mid-abyss, their many, torn and truncated root-arms outstretched, with enough bouyancy to not sink further through the liquid soil, and enough network spread in their severed, subterranean limbs to catch and hold each other and the fill that poured down on them from above. After two years of work, the landfill level had risen ten feet above the water.

Odd, to be talking about the difficulty of finding bedrock in a place that has the exposed rock of the Niagara Escarpment in full and constant view. It's as though our foundation is above ground, not below. Bedrock does exist under Mercer's Glen, Cootes Paradise and the Iroquois Bar, but by last count it's two hundred metres down. Dundas Valley is indeed much like an earth-version of the Niagara Gorge, with hills instead of water pouring through it. But it turns out that this gorge is significantly deeper than Niagara's, and filled to the brim with debris the glaciers carried down in ice ages prior to the one that shaped the landscape we see, filled with the stuff their rivers carried along and deposited, and topped with a plush mattress of the pollen, seeds, leaves, weeds and clippings of seasons-millennial. The glacier and water-carved world we inhabit here above is nothing to the work that's buried below. We float over an earth disassembled. I expect the Bar almost to have a little spring underfoot, to bounce when jumped on.

Johnny Mercer had known about the Desjardins canal, and was equally familiar with the railway and the origins of the Glen. The soil was very fertile in the Mercers' corner of Cootes Paradise, full of worms, and to Johnny's mind this fertility had to do with the weight of the landfill forcing up the rich, organic ooze from the marsh bottom. A patch of land at the end of their lane, past the third house, was large enough to farm, and Mr. Johnson, who owned the first farm on the right up Old Guelph Road, would come down with his tractor and plow the plot for them in exchange for some of the food they grew. In addition to the vegetables and corn, Johnny said they also had various fruit trees to pick from, and there were always fish swimming in the pond, looking for a hook.

*We never went hungry.*

The cul-de-sac created by the landfill embankment was separated from the body of the marsh by the low embankment of the old Old Guelph Road. George and Emily Mercer were part of the gradual influx of people that began living in the area around and after the turn of the century. It was often a case of temporary, job-related shelter becoming permanent. Many of the first residents worked on the crews for the construction of the new railway of 1895, the various cuts through the Bar, the new bridges the railways required, or, in George Senior's case, the bridge for the Hamilton-Toronto Highway. When the jobs ended, the people stayed.

Others came for the same reasons the first ones stayed, because it was a less expensive place to live than the city, and beside water. The railway owned the land around the canal cut, and leased to the boathouse dwellers at rates considerably lower than the property taxes they would have paid in the city. The Mercers were unusual in that they owned their property.

But while the primary mode of transportation for one century, the railway, created Mercer's Glen, the primary mode of the next—the six-lane, limited access highway—unmade it.

When the route for a new highway into the city was being planned in the 1940s and 50s, several options were on the table. The provincial ministry in charge of the project had their local office in Rasberry House, a large farmhouse a short way up Old Guelph Road from the Mercers', on the north shore of Cootes Paradise. Old Guelph climbs a headland between two ravines on the north shore. On the right is the ravine that empties into Mercer's Glen, on the left a ravine that separated Rasberry House from the road. To get to Rasberry House, ministry officials had to travel farther up the road and skirt around the end of this ravine. In anticipation of a highway route that would bridge the entire, ravine-riven north shore, and make getting to work simpler, a causeway was landfilled across the ravine, linking Rasberry House directly to Old Guelph Road.

Johnny Mercer vividly remembered the bulldozers working that job, as does Margaret Brunton. It riles them both, still. The stomping ground of their childhood was beginning to be destroyed. The landfill causeway prevented the two of them from walking up the ravine from the marsh to collect the berries that grew at the head of the ravine. They would bring the berries to a woman who lived in one of the boathouses by the canal, who baked them into pies.

The highway was planned to go through Dundas Valley, filling in the shoreline ravines as it went, taking advantage of the break in the wall of the Niagara Escarpment that the valley provided. Geographically, remember, Hamilton is avoidable—you have to *want* to get here. The highway was taking the path of least resistance, which was up the valley, but thereby skirting the city, which felt bypassed. Pressure was exerted to bring the highway into and through the city instead, along the marsh shoreline of the Bar, much like the pressure that Allan MacNab exerted to have the railway come into town along the bay shore of the Bar. This time the mayor and city council were behind the push. Like MacNab in his day, the city had its way.

Chedoke highway, the 403, now enters the basin of Cootes Paradise by bursting through the railway embankment behind the Mercers' old place. It rides on a bed of landfill ten metres high, burying the third house at the end of their laneway, their small acreage, half the pond, and almost every inch of the Bruntons' large property. The Bruntons' house was torn down. Had it been left standing, their two-and-a-half storeys of brick would be buried to about the height of the chimney. I think of that chimney top anyway, when I drive over the highway, as a square rabbit hole covered by a sewer grate, leading down to a furnace that is the basement antechamber of the buried world of their home.

Scotty Brunton had died in 1960, but Mrs. Brunton still lived in the house, and was forced to move to the city, when the Gardens sold her property to the province for the highway. The Mercers were expropriated. It must have been a challenge to assess the market value of the Mercer property and homes. Johnny's father had long ago told the family that the highway would be coming through, and encouraged his sons to hold out for as much money as they could possibly squeeze from provincial coffers. Three of Johnny's brothers were still living at the Glen when the ministry came calling in the early 1960s.

I asked Johnny, "What did they hold out for?"

"They probably got enough for three cases of beer. That would have been all they wanted," said Johnny.

The highway ran into the same problem as the railway with the marsh's bottomlessness, but took a different approach to the solution. Instead of trying to landfill the abyss, they removed it. A giant hose was slung across the old Old Guelph Road. One end of the hose was set in the marsh, the other in the small pond of Mercer's Glen. The marsh bottom was then pumped into the pond. Over the course of a few months, the rich, organic mud sank out of sight, joining the marble tiles, bicycles and tree stumps, but eventually the pond water was displaced as the mud level rose to more or less the same as the water level of the marsh. The pumped-out area of the marsh was then filled with more stable material to provide a bed for the highway.

Meanwhile, naturalists at the Royal Botanical Gardens were on pins and needles to see what would happen next, for seeds that had fallen into the marsh hundreds of years ago and lain dormant were now exposed to daylight.

WHAT REMAINS OF MERCER'S GLEN today is a brief glimpse

*Mercer's Glen*

from Chedoke highway, leaving or entering the city. From the driver's seat, the high, quaking aspens surrounding the Glen, the bulrushes standing in water, seem intended, garden-like. You'd never dream people once lived down there. In dry years, you'd never dream a connection existed between that small area of bulrushes and aspen, and Cootes Paradise on the other side. In wet years, the Glen's patchy sheet of water provides a visual connection between the two, but you still wouldn't dream the two were once one body.

That sheet of water reflecting the sky is deceptively thin, of course. A thin sheet is all that is required, though, if the temperature drops below zero. When it does, and the sheet freezes over, the shoulders of Old Guelph Road where George and Al and I parked our vehicles become jammed with cars with license plates that read "OPA," and other German-language equivalents for the retired or semi-retired. The grandfathers are out (*Opa* means "grandpa"), playing their version of the sport of curling, which involves heavy flat disks, with a handle sticking straight up from the middle of each one. They climb the embankment of the old Old Guelph Road onto the Glen, and clear a lane or two between the bulrushes. Their network rivals the one birders have set up for unusual sightings. You have to take immediate advantage of freezing conditions around here, because conditions won't last.

The German grandfathers were not out the time George and Johnny and I visited the Glen in early winter. We'd gone to check out a view of the point where Johnny and Margaret and their friends swung from the willow. The point is the only portion of the Bruntons' property not buried under highway. Nipped off, it still pokes into Cootes Paradise. We were standing in the tunnel under the highway, looking straight at the side of the Iroquois Bar.

Johnny pointed and said, "There it is: the path Scotty Brunton used to take to work every day."

So it was, clearly visible under a thin layer of snow, ascending on an easy diagonal from the bottom to the top of the Bar.

Sometimes all you need is a little distance, and a little snow. Snow that covers the earth not in forgetfulness but in remembrance—someone should write a poem. The white descends, and shapes in the landscape otherwise hidden emerge, are revealed, as was the Lover's Lane remnant of old-old-Old Guelph Road.

I look for Scotty's path now each time I travel through the tunnel on my way home from work. When the leaves are on the trees, the path is completely obscured. During the autumn, winter and early spring I can see it, sometimes, even without a thin layer of white. The path seems to have the ability to move in and out of visibility, depending on conditions that remain mysterious, and don't last. Perhaps its visibility depends on the path's own desire to be seen, the earth's desire to show it.

It may be beyond presumption to make claims for the earth's desire, but I've become willing to think that it is the earth's prerogative to show these traces when it chooses, and that the earth does choose. I drove to and from work all those hundreds and thousands of times before the landscape began to impress itself upon me and the questions began to form that eventually lifted my behind-the-wheel blindness. The landscape itself woke and made me willing and wishing to see beyond the scenery, to read the lines of the storied shapes and contours I was passing through. It might just as well have continued to withhold that sight. I take no credit. You try to keep awake once you've been roused. You hope to have eyes open wide enough to catch the earth's small remembrances as they're given. But it's hit and miss.

My daughter, the one of the "valuable junk," has come along to Mercer's Glen. "What a dump," she says, and I feel a pang. She's right. It's hard to argue, up close, once you stop the car and walk around. Mercer's Glen today is one of those spots where a devotion to moving through the landscape on four wheels, the demands placed on it by that devotion, has created a landscape best experienced from a distance, as scenery. The place feels discarded: organic compost dump for the Gardens, dump for the flying litter and hubcaps from the highway, dump for the landfilled beds of railway and road. Mercer's Glen now serves purposes—and places—outside of itself.

In trying to respond to my daughter's dismissal, her distress, I wonder if I've become desensitized to the destruction myself, if the layers of change have also buried me. How does one develop, explain, affection for a place so put-upon? I love it for the view that explodes into sight as I exit the tunnel under Chedoke highway on the way home from work. I love it for the hands-on-the-wheel way the road curves, dips down, touches where water level was, and immediately rises out again, always curving. I love it even though, or perhaps because, it is much beaten and abandoned. I love it to override the fact it's a dump. I love the natural folds and shapes—overlaid, altered, by human-made shapes which compete in scale with the original work—that have let me into their secret. I love it for the Mercers, the Bruntons, the boathouse dwellers, who lived their routines here in an everyday, physical relation to the place as a place, a home; for their walking up, over, around its natural and not-so natural features, every square inch, lives lived about and by the open wound, or here at the dammed outlet. Their sleeping against the Bar's side. I love their traces, the shards of roadways and paths, Scotty's path, Lover's Lane, that restore, enhance, gentle the roughness with which the place has been handled; that take the side of the landscape and compete against, even undo, the overbearing physical alterations. That heal. This is my version of the twelve-year-old's outburst of affection for Albion Falls, sung in perfect knowledge of the toll the landscape has paid, pays.

GEORGE AND AL AND I stood at the base of the railway embankment, using the sun and stars of their own stories to take their bearings, to reach as close as possible the spot where Granny's house stood. We were part of the view for the cars passing on the highway. The brothers looked for the apple tree that stood just outside Granny's door, talked about fishing in the pond and on the marsh. Al claimed that his older brother forced him to sit those long spells in a boat. They talked about being city kids with a country home to visit whenever they wanted, about other city kids envying the ones who lived on the marsh or the bay, or by the canal. Cootes as kid's paradise.

Another willow tree stood beside the canal under the High Level Bridge. George placed his hands on Al's face and showed me the scar above the eye, which Al received in a mid-air collision with another boy while swinging on a rope tied to a branch that hung over the water. Al had fallen into the canal after the collision.

Al's initial suspicion about my motivation seemed to have vanished during our walk and conversation. Perhaps he had wondered if I was trying to lay claim to a place that, by right of Grandmother Mercer and a youth spent in her precincts, truly was his. It had been claimed-away once before. Both he and George had remained living in the general area, but the landscape they'd grown up in had been taken from under the Mercer family's feet, then filled and buried out of existence. They'd been dispossessed, then made strangers to their home landscape, forced to feel that they didn't belong. Resident aliens.

It turned out the brothers were resident alien by blood, too. Al mentioned that he and George were finally getting around to applying for their status cards as First Nations people. Their mother had been native.

Al still had in his hand the takeout coffee cup from Tim Hortons. He and George and both their wives had all carried cups when they'd emerged from their trucks an hour or two earlier. Finishing his cigarette, Al dropped the butt into the mouth-hole in the cup's lid. Its lit end hit the leftover coffee at the bottom with a quick *fssst*, dead. He then reached over my left shoulder and in what struck me as a moment of surprising intimacy, wedged the cup into the crotch of a small tree standing behind me, and we headed back to our vehicles.

# The stuff we're made of

THE CAR IS ALREADY CLIMBING as it exits the tunnel under Chedoke highway, past Mercer's Glen. Curving as it climbs the north shore of Cootes Paradise, it finds and follows the ridge between ravines. The depth of the ravines, the steepness of their sides and the narrowness of the ridge itself, are really only apparent in winter when the leaves are down. In summer, traffic drives through an opening in the crowns of northern red oaks rooted to slopes slanted at forty-five degrees. The trees lessen the possible vertigo.

The ride is brief. From the Glen to the foot of the Niagara Escarpment it's two kilometres across the width of this narrow strip of land, this raised beach of glacial Lake Iroquois.

The beach is riven by many ravines as deep and steep as the two that Old Guelph Road rides between. Halfway to the escarpment the ravines run out, their vees disappear, subsumed into a rolling landscape, some of which is farmland, some taken up by small subdivision, single home or family cemetery. The land rises and falls in gently lulling, oceanic swells. If landscapes suggest each their own notion of time, this one suggests that it is possible and desirable to enter time. The hills move and gather their school of whalebacks unnoticed, hiding and guiding the dip that runs between them, and into which they direct all melting and fallen water. The dip deepens, then takes on a life of its own and plunges down toward the marsh shoreline, cutting through the soil like a huge knife.

The ravines attest to something sudden, short-lived, and of tremendous velocity, though the water that made them runs through at a relative trickle now, or only after rain, or in spring. These streams are one on the list of the various ways in which water has shaped the landscape: bulldozing glaciers, bar-making waves, bar-carving meltwater currents, rock-gnawing rivers, ravine-riving runoff. Driving the glacial lake bed, the time you enter is the same geographical short-term—the most recent, and relatively brief, land-shaping period—that also sent the Iroquois Bar into retirement. It was twelve or thirteen thousand years ago that a new path to the Atlantic opened for Lake Iroquois, and its level dropped thirty metres, overnight. Water slashed through the landscape in its haste to the ocean.

All in all, the beach and ravines are a compact example of late ice-age landscaping. A public earthwork's project under the direction of Matt Broman's great-grandfather, so to speak—an ancestor in Oriah's sense of the word. He must have been a giant. The two-lane blacktop, yet unimproved, clings to this craftwork, follows all curves, riding the solid, slow-motion waves of earth.

We find ourselves living the long pause between incredibly stretched-out episodes of an ongoing event.

HALFWAY FROM SHORELINE to escarpment, Old Guelph Road comes to a four-way stop. One day my friend Bernadette and I parked the car near the four-way, and slipped and slid to the bottom of a ravine—neither of the two that the road goes between, but a third ravine—hanging onto and bending small trees on the slope as we went. Because it was muddy and we'd be walking in water, we wore rubber boots. Our plan was to follow the ravine to its mouth, where it emptied into the landlocked pond, the former channel around the end of the Iroquois Bar, between the two railway embankments.

An exploratory adventure. A mild, mid-spring jaunt. We'd planned the outing for some time already, but I was surprised at my own high level of anticipation. Eager, positively bouncy. Or as Mary put it, "It's spring; your sap is running."

This far up the beach the ravine is more like a valley. It hasn't yet begun its knife-like plunge to the shore, and so its sides are not high. The stream meanders along the bottom, with enough flat land on both sides to graze animals or grow fruit trees. Many of the ravines, in their valley portions, once were farmed. Some still have remnant fruit trees growing, old and wild. If Bernadette and I had looked before we slipped and slid, we could have followed a tractor path down. We noticed its gentle grade against the side of the valley as we walked along, the stream burbling within earshot, the valley walls seeming to grow higher with each step we took.

Closing in, too. The walls were funnelling us, reducing arable land and pushing us to walk closer to the stream, though not yet in it. Within a few hundred metres we found ourselves up against a third wall, as high as the two walls of the valley itself, that turned the valley into a cul-de-sac.

Shades of Mercer's Glen: it was the landfill embankment of a railway crossing the valley. At first it looked as though we had no choice but to go over the top of the embankment, and had climbed halfway up the path before noticing that the stream entered a culvert. A concrete culvert, shaped to a gothic point at its peak. We wondered if we could follow it through the embankment.

Bent double, we could. With our backs up against the cold concrete of the tunnel's peak, under tons of earth and railway, heads cocked at an awkward angle to see the way ahead, shuffling and splashing through the water in our rubber boots, and trusting that the dot of daylight at the other end wouldn't diminish but grow larger, large enough for us to squeeze through.

The tunnel was longer than it looked, and the damp chill dug deeper into us the deeper into it we walked, or waddled. I said to Bernadette that it reminded me of the old railway tunnel in town that I had recently walked the length of, which was also damp and cold and much longer than it looked, long enough to become scary, but at least you could walk upright through it. She said that except for the temperature, it reminded her of being born.

The dot of daylight did grow, and finally, with a rush of warmer, humid spring air, we were freed and found ourselves standing in a shallow pool of water fed by the stream that was falling over the lip of the culvert. After a few moments' recovery, we turned to see from whence we had come. A date was chiselled into the concrete of the gothic point above our exit: 1911.

"The year my mother was born," said Bernadette. She'd

missed by a generation. We'd gone further back than we thought.

Our mid-spring venture took on a sense of grander drama then, a scale that our physical surroundings complemented. On this side of the railway embankment, the sides of the valley were markedly higher. No longer a valley but a true ravine, its cleft cut so deeply and steeply into the earth there was room only for the stream's tight meander at the bottom. The slopes themselves were unexpectedly monochromatic, red, with occasional layers of very pale green, and looked more like piled soil, compressed into hardness, than rock. Tall, narrow northern red oak and maple grew on these steep slopes, slopes otherwise bare of any undergrowth. The trees stretched their trunks and limbs to clear the ravine's rim, the green of their leaves also very pale, and sparse, and high above.

We splashed along the stream bottom, frankly awestruck to find such scenery so close to home, and to be within it, to be touching and brushing against the water-carved walls, or staring down at and stepping on the alternating layers of red and grey-green that lay exposed in liquid brightness on the stream bed. The walls and stream bed were shale, the stuff of the Appalachian mountains, I later learned: the deep alluvial bed of rivers that wore the Appalachians down and carried them away, westward, depositing them here in ages of water and ice that preceded Lake Iroquois. We were walking a liquid path through disassembled mountains.

Our stream's gradient took us along with it, carrying us down through ranges of time before our mothers and grandmothers were born, over short falls, taking us deeper into the past, courtesy of the water that had built and shaped and reshaped this landscape from day one, the same water, cycled and recycled, that splashed our boots as we walked this one spring day. Water the living presence of the past that surrounded us.

We came to a place where the ravine turned and a second, steep-sided ravine joined it. By now we'd progressed far, and deeply, and the slanted walls were almost at their highest. Looking up at those huge, twin red vees, and the prow of red headland that separated them, at how the two ravines melded to become one, it suddenly struck me how someone in a creative frame of mind might have gotten the idea for another kind of other shaping, while standing rapt before one like this.

"So *that's* it. That's why. It's because *we're made of this stuff.*"

I laughed. Loudly. Maniacally, Bernadette said later. It gave her a bit of a fright. She was a few metres back and out of sight when she heard my outburst, had wondered whether or not to worry and hurried to catch up. But these realizations come when you least expect and can tip your usual balance. I had wondered why permanent, human changes to the landscape had such a visceral effect on me: the landfills, the suburban hill-levelling, the re-engineering of geographies for railways and six-lane highways. Why did I sometimes feel that I had to close my eyes and walk and talk *around* these physical changes, ignore them, in order to be able to walk and talk at all? The damage hurt, hurt physically. It's as though it had been done to me—a notion that always seemed stretching the issue.

Here, suddenly, was the connection. It *had* been done to

me. Because *we're made from this stuff;* this earth, this shale, this mud and suffering clay.

Me *and thee*, I said to Bernadette. She wasn't nearly as taken by the revelation, as I fumbled through trying to communicate an explanation there and then. I was in the pre-articulate stage of discovery, still laughing. She was still powerfully teed-off with the garbage dumped into the ravine, the tires in the water. That's what had slowed her down.

Together we continued wading deeper through the millennia, she with her righteous indignation, the kind that leads to phone calls, letters, action, and me with my big-picture, which on a good day will lead to this, what I am doing now, which may not change a damn thing. All the while I was recalling the story I'd heard countless times as a child, about the first earthly couple being fashioned from clay and water, mud-pie style, and all they needed for their vivification, for life, was the enspiriting breath of spring. They were the very soil they walked upon. This was the first time that ancestor-story had really hit home.

The atmosphere in the ravine began to change noticeably. A more luxuriant air, warm and humid and, well, pregnant, invaded and overcame the cool dampness of water and rock that had surrounded us for the last hour. The ravine began to widen. We stepped out of the stream, having walking room on the bank again. The canopy of pale green high above us became the foliage surrounding us, and the sunlight was no longer filtered, but direct. The ravine walls spread open like arms ready to give or receive and we felt as though we were about to be delivered into whatever world the earth, water and air had created for us. Given the build-up, we expected Eden.

Even though I knew what was coming, it was still a slap in the face. Eden was on the other side of another wall, a larger version of the railway landfill embankment that we'd encountered earlier. Larger—higher, longer—because here the ravine was much deeper and wider, and this causeway carried six lanes of Chedoke highway. We could hear the traffic roaring overtop of the ravine's walled-shut mouth.

And no dot of daylight beckoned at the far end of the galvanized culvert that carried the stream under the barrier into the landlocked pond, the pond that was the former channel around the end of the Iroquois Bar. We laboured up a path that took us to the rim of the ravine, but didn't even consider crossing the six lanes to see what we were missing on the other side. Our afternoon adventure was over. We stood beside the guardrail on the highway shoulder and watched the cars whip past like the flaming sword-swings of cherubim, barring the way.

# Mr. McQuestion

"You've changed. You're fatter," she said.

"It's the beer. I love the beer. In fact I was going to pick up a six-pack on the way home today," was his reply.

She had been the housekeeping wife of a man fully employed. Together, husband and wife had raised two children on the shore of Cootes Paradise. One of those children, Margaret, now grown, also sat in the room.

He, of the six-pack, was Margaret's peer and former playmate, the son of a man who lost gainful employment before this son was even born. Johnny couldn't be absolutely sure that a work-related injury ended George Mercer Senior's working days, but he was certain that ever since the day he, Johnny, was born, his dad never had a job. In the community around the canal and the marsh, that fact did not set him apart.

When Johnny first told me about Scotty climbing the path every day to work at the Rock Garden, and the Brunton family living across Old Guelph Road from the Mercers, beside the marsh, I looked up their name in the phone book, too. There weren't many to choose from. The first call was taken by a Mrs. M. Brunton.

"Oh yes, Graham was my husband. Everyone else called him Scotty," she said.

People just go on living here. Mrs. Brunton was now ninety-seven years old, and living in the high-rise apartment building that she had moved into thirty-five years earlier after being dislocated by the highway. She warmed to the topic immediately, relating details about living and raising children on the shore of Cootes Paradise as though she'd been waiting for someone to ask. Her first words about the place echoed George Mercer's words about the spring at the Glen, the "coolest, clearest, sweetest-tasting water" he'd ever had.

"I loved every minute that we lived by the marsh," she said. "Every minute. And I regretted ever having to leave."

MRS. BRUNTON RECALLED Johnny as a child spying through the bushes at their house in what she understood to be envy, and she remembered her husband Graham coming home with a pair of secondhand skates for Johnny, Johnny's first pair. Johnny himself could recall neither event. On the day that he and I went with Margaret to visit her mother, Margaret Senior and the neighbour boy hadn't seen each other in nearly forty years. It wouldn't have taken many pounds for him to be noticeably fatter now than in adolescence or youth, but in any event Johnny was unrepentant. He gave the distinct impression that if he'd been living with his three older brothers at the time of their expropriation from the Glen, the Ministry of Highways would have had to cough up at least one more case of beer.

Mrs. Brunton moved out of her home because the Ministry was expropriating that property as well. The Bruntons had been living on parkland, essentially, during the decades when all of Cootes Paradise and its surrounding shoreline, as well as the Burlington Heights half of the Iroquois Bar, was slowly being turned over to public rather than private interests.

City politician Thomas B. McQuesten had had a large hand in the ongoing effort. He'd gone on a years-long land-buying spree as a member of the city Parks Board. When the Board's budget money became insufficient to buy all the property he felt was needed for parkland, he invented another vehicle for land acquisition and maintenance, and by the 1930s the Royal Botanical Gardens was born. The Gardens had owned the Bruntons property for more than thirty years when the Ministry laid their wide highway hands on it.

Everyone in the room was familiar with McQuesten, whom they all called "Mr. McQuestion." The familiarity, however, could not have been called affectionate. To this day, people in general show an ambivalence toward the man that this mispronunciation of his name succinctly expresses. The ambivalence stems partly from the fact that he was an influential, determined, and very public politician, with a highly developed sense of civic responsibility, who happened also to be a lawyer living in a big stone house, Whitehern, in the centre of the city. He exuded privilege, though in fact his personal wealth was not especially great.

The ambivalence also comes from the fact that Mr. McQuestion had been a driving force behind the dismantling of the boathouse community that had grown up around the canal cut. The beautification of Burlington Heights—with sunken memorial gardens, a reflecting pool, ornamental plantings—the building of the High Level Bridge, the development of York Road into a four-lane boulevard bordered by public parkland, and the construction of a new four-lane road along the marsh shoreline, over the canal and up the Heights, had been accomplished at the expense of the entire canal population.

As a child, McQuesten himself had learned first-hand the effect that lines of transportation can have on the landscape. In his case, the railway taught the lesson—the same railway that gave birth to the boathouse community. The community began when workers constructing a third railway across Burlington Heights in 1895 built temporary shelters for themselves beside the canal. The first railway, in the 1850s, had helped render the canal obsolete as a commercial waterway, as railways did to canals all over North America, so there was no one to mind these shelters being built, or to mind when they became permanent after the job was done. Others soon were attracted to the location.

Backed by a city plebiscite in which neighbouring wards approved the plan, and exercising its own commercial privilege, the new railway entered the city first through a poorer neighbourhood, and then through the wealthy area that included Whitehern. Much of the wealthy neighbourhood was insulated from the effects because the homes stood on top of the Iroquois Bar, and the train travelled beneath them through a new tunnel. Whitehern, by contrast, stood beside the Bar, not on top. The mouth of the tunnel opened onto its backyard. The train, in fact, ran between the house and the Presbyterian church that McQuesten's father had helped construct, effectively separating the two buildings.

No amount of privilege or politicking by the McQuesten family or any other of the well-placed residents of the neighbourhood was able to prevent it. The entire episode, as well as later struggles against the railway, made a big impression on young Thomas B.—he was thirteen years old when the tracks were laid. The high stone wall that still surrounds Whitehern's backyard helped to block the sight of the railway, and muffle some of the noise. The wall was built with money the family received for the expropriation of its property.

Within a couple of years of the tunnel's completion, the first automobile arrived from a factory in Ohio at the station one block from the McQuesten home, drawing crowds of people. By the 1920s, it was already clear that this object of intense public curiosity stood on the verge of becoming a universal conveyance that would also reshape the landscape, as the railways had. McQuesten saw it coming and wanted to get there first, to exercise some control over how that reshaping took place, to mesh the use of the car, and its engineering requirements in terms of roadways and bridges, with the aesthetics of an urban landscape.

A larger, continental parks movement was underway at the time, but McQuesten's experience in the backyard of Whitehern provided a good part of the impetus behind his work to establish what the city takes such pride in now: the parks below and along the brow of the escarpment, Albion Falls and King's Forest, Mountain Brow Boulevard, Cootes Paradise and the Royal Botanical Gardens. Personally, I tend to be unambivalent about the man.

Ultimately, McQuesten wasn't the only reason for the boathouse community's demise. The new roadways, gardens and parkland along the top of Burlington Heights were meant to bless, and contain, the blossoming population of cars. But cars are democratic, almost levelling, you might say. More people could move around more often, farther and in more directions than before, and were able to observe much more of the landscape. During that period, large numbers of people first experienced Sunday driving, and began noticing the countryside. There are some wonderful stories about early driving excursions, the rapture over scenery viewed for the first time, drives over new bridges where the writers comment on a prospect on the landscape not available before. You get the impression these drivers simply stopped their cars, got out, and stepped over to the rail to gawk. As a result of all this scenic viewing, their landscape on display, localities began to spruce up their surroundings and natural attractions. The view from the heights, and the bridge over the Desjardins canal-cut, was very pretty—if you kept your head up. Down below were the boathouses.

During the civic debate on the fate of the boathouse community, some public sentiment was expressed in favour of allowing the residents to keep their homes. One city councillor in particular thought it unconscionable to unhouse people during an economic depression. Others considered the area a ramshackle eyesore, its residents a drain on the public purse, its children marshrats. "Marshrat" was the name children commonly took home to the canal from school in the city—schools their parents paid no taxes to support because the boathouses stood on land leased from the railway.

The stigma of poverty and non-compliance attached itself to the community, though a number of residents had full-time work in the city as trolley-drivers and firemen. Some made a living off the water itself, fishing, or as guides. When the city pressured the railway into turning over to it the land under their homes, the railway complied and eviction notices went out.

*Mr. McQuestion*

The injustice rankles, on the one hand, and it seems that an idyllic life at waterside was given the boot simply because it wasn't up to the imposed standards of a mobile middle class, but the boathouse community's days may have been numbered anyway. Along with the nineteenth-century railways came the industrialization that was slowly overwhelming the bay's ability to absorb and disperse pollution. Sewer systems replaced outdoor privies in the city, but their pipes emptied into creeks, the bay, and into Cootes Paradise. Johnny Mercer and his friends had their own name for Chedoke Creek: Shit Creek.

Warnings about health hazards began to be heard quite early in the century, but it took a long time for people to come to believe water could be an enemy, and to turn their backs on it. They swam and fished as long as they could. Some remember, still, playing and splashing and jumping from the top rim of the wide-open mouth of an outflow pipe into, well, into it. No doubt they were yodelling variations on the theme sung by the twelve-year-old at Albion Falls as they sailed through the air. Swimming wasn't officially prohibited until the 1940s, and only recently has it tentatively, on some days, at very specific locations in the bay, been allowed again because of hard-won water improvements.

By the end of the 1930s, most members of the boathouse community had moved away, their homes demolished or moved. Some residents held out, resisting as long as they could. One man barricaded himself in his house against the oncoming bulldozers. He stepped out for a moment one day thinking the coast was clear, but returned to find the house levelled. A delegation of women walked together downtown to City Hall, where they hoped to talk the sheriff into stopping the destruction of their homes and community. They were counting on their strength in numbers as wives and mothers, but their brief interview knocked the last little wind of hope out of their sails. Returning home to the canal, one of the women stopped at a house on York Street to rent rooms for herself and her family.

The changes of the 1930s did not affect the Mercers or the Bruntons because their corner of the world was removed from the canal. Their eviction came later, with the generation of roads that came after the Second World War, and the limited-access highway. In between, Thomas McQuesten had moved out of the civic and into the provincial political scene, broadening his sphere. As the Minister of Highways for the provincial government, he initiated the development of parkland in and around Niagara Falls, and the construction of the Niagara Parkway, rescuing the landscape along the Canadian side of the Niagara River from the kind of development that took place on the American side. The British Army forts on the Niagara and St. Lawrence Rivers were restored and opened as tourist attractions under his tenure, and he oversaw the design and building of the province's first limited-access highway, the Queen Elizabeth Way, with its boulevard-like feel and bridges adorned with commissioned sculpture—though the effects have been mostly lost now to increased traffic and road widenings.

Someone in the same ministerial position that McQuesten occupied made the decisions that led to the Chedoke highway, which was constructed after McQuesten's retirement. I wonder now what difference it would have made to the shoreline of Cootes Paradise coming into Hamilton had McQuesten still been in charge.

## Mr. McQuestion

MARGARET SENIOR, Margaret, Johnny and I were talking about life beside the marsh, from a perch high above the downtown, in one of the multi-storeyed honeycombs of concrete that replaced many of the large, old homes on the estate-size lots that once graced the top of the Iroquois Bar. Margaret Senior moved into this building when she left Cootes Paradise. At the same time as the Chedoke highway was being constructed, developers were turning what had been a neighbourhood of the few into a precinct of the many. Whitehern was spared, deeded to the city after Thomas McQuesten's death, and like Alexander MacNab's home, Dundurn Castle, it became a museum.

In the atmosphere of tension that existed between those who lived beside Cootes Paradise and the forces—cultural and political—that swept their community from its shore, McQuesten inevitably was made out to be something of a villain.

Margaret Brunton—mother and daughter—and Johnny Mercer, recalled that each summer a large, black car could be seen making the turn from York Boulevard onto Old Guelph Road—*old* Old Guelph Road. It would follow the road down toward the canal and the community where the Duckworths lived, and the Hazels, the Coopers, Lashmores and Glennies. Babe Bennett. Someone should write a book. Johnny once told a story about walking to school one day with a friend and hearing a scream coming from the canal as they crossed the bridge. They ran and looked over the rail. A man with bloody hands came out of the quonset home directly below them. The man was Babe. He climbed into a boat and rowed to the other side of the canal. Soon he was crossing the canal again with a second person. The two went into the quonset. Johnny later found out that a baby had been born.

The big black car would make a hairpin, right-hand turn when it reached the bottom of the old Old Guelph Road, and drive along the marsh shoreline, past the last boathouse before the Brunton's property line, Husky Reid's place (Reid was a fireman and former football player with the Tigers, a team that later joined with the Wildcats to become the Hamilton Tiger Cats), and past the budding lilac dell that Scotty had planted and that was beginning to attract people, and their cars, by the hundreds.

The car would turn into the Bruntons' driveway and stop by the water, at the boatshed. Two men in dark suits emerged.

"They always wore their suits."

One of the men carried a heavy briefcase of civic ambition and accomplishment. A recognizable public figure. The other travelled light, could have been anyone. Mr. McQuestion and friend. Matt Broman? McQuesten's brother, Calvin? Calvin had as much difficulty with steady employment as did Johnny Mercer's father, and had returned to living at home. He spent a good deal of his time around the marsh. Whoever the second was, both gentlemen from the inner reaches of the city were under the observation of the woman of the house, and a couple of children hiding in the bushes.

"They came every summer. At least once."

There is something here about treating the landscape as special, as worth preserving within the urban context and for its own sake, about retaining a sense of seeing it for the first time. About renewing that sense. Which I think is what these two men were up to.

There is also something about his feeling of ownership with regards to the landscape: theirs by right of citizenship, responsibility and, if one may be so bold, love. The two men had that, too—and rightly so, it could be argued.

Mr. McQuestion and a friend pull a canoe from the Brunton shed and launch their annual tool about Paradise.

As for the ones watching, and the others who live here and will be displaced, or who already have been displaced, whether they rent or lease, or whether their housing comes with the job, for them there is something else. In their relation to the place, in the intimacy of their daily contact, moving within the precincts of Bar, bay and marsh, they *possess*, to quote poet Richard Wilbur once more, *what the owners can but own.*

## *Blondin on a Tightrope* ❧

The light is such that wire shines
arches upside down
                            post by post
loping along the shining road.

From the celebration of the Falls
a current of excitement lasts
till beyond the town ahead
                            where
it will stand houses round its maypole
make clothing in the Maytag dance
and keep the population up
                            past dark.

If we were at Niagara now
we could see where this business begins
There it is all rock
                      water    rock
and the water's great
                            exaggerated fall
A change in elevation's one thing
but Lord, the volume of it
                            uncontained.

In June of 1859
Blondin on a tightrope
                            crossed the gorge
For eighteen minutes

he held the crowd
                    suspended
in an air of hopeless disbelief
                                    Water
turned white
Men fainted
Women wept
                when, almost over
the hero performed a backward somersault
He stepped at last onto the dry ground
                        of their thunderous applause
and minutes later, fortified by celebration and
champagne, and not just a little bit nuts
he scamped the way back like a squirrel
crossing the wire in seven
                                And that summer
did the same thing over
                    but blindfold
                    on bicycle
                    & behind a barrow
They came from all over, to be contained
in the power of the place and because
of the man's outrageous stunts.

Sometimes along this stretch
men climb the trunk
of a telephone pole
                        like it was every day
They go to play tricks
                    on the currency
to fix the stream

                         that rides the wire
that comes from somewhere
                    deep inside the gorge
that strides in strict formation
                    above the earth
                    beside the King's #6
     assuming the countryside.

Here on Millgrove Road, looking east
at 8 a.m.
                    angles of the sun
electrify the air
                    the bright dominion
reveals shade
                    delivers lines
of radiant particularity
                    across the yard
to house and barn
And from the porcelain hold
          a commotion of electrons
is orderly dispersed.

# Where Here Is

HERE IS NOT FAR FROM Niagara Falls. Niagara and the Iroquois Bar are related to each other. The waterfall is the younger, celebrity sibling of the pair, but they're family, geographically speaking.

You can get here from there.

And vice versa. The last time we travelled to Niagara Falls, Mary and I went together, alone. It's an hour away by car, and we decided to do the whole tour this time: drive the length of the Niagara Parkway south from where it begins at the Niagara River's mouth at Lake Ontario, along the river through the fruit land below the Niagara Escarpment, then up the escarpment and along the top edge of the Niagara Gorge until we reached Niagara Falls itself, after which we would travel on to the river's source at Lake Erie. A sixty-kilometre drive—the Niagara is a short river—more or less divided equally into those three distinct parts.

We were feeling right at home as we drove along the Parkway and its well-appointed route; it's like family, too. This brainchild of Thomas B. McQuesten still retains some of its pre-War, Driving Tour feel, which encourages and rewards a take-your-time, take-it-all-in approach.

I've wondered if the phrase "North America's love affair with the car" was coined during that pre-War period. It would make sense for people to fall instantly and deeply in love with a means of conveyance that could show so many so much of the world, with so little effort. The phrase implies an infidelity, as though people were enjoying an intimate relationship with an inanimate object, the car, a relationship more stimulating and exciting, more thrilling, and that carried with it an edge of danger, than the relationship it was breaking. And the relationship being broken? I would guess it was the one between the person and the place where they parked the car each night.

The Parkway passes through the small town of Queenston at the base of the escarpment, climbs, and once atop the escarpment sticks pretty closely to the edge of the river canyon, the Niagara Gorge, or, as the road signs put it, The Gorge. Outside the driver's window is a seventy-metre sheer drop. The matching wall of the opposite side of the canyon is visible, and there are occasional, brief sightings of The River below, its intense, liquid muscle unwillingly confined by the rock on both sides. The Whirlpool, where the muscle turns on itself. These features are all duly noted by the signs, with first letters capitalized and articles definite.

Approaching and entering the city of Niagara Falls, houses begin to line the pavement out the passenger window: family dwellings, bed and breakfasts, front porches with wicker furniture and national flags. They're feeling right at home too, front windows staring out and over The Gorge as placidly as though the houses were looking into the windows of brick kin across the street, rather than into the abyss. You grow blasé, even in a life-threatening geography. Perhaps even more blasé, as a kind of compensation. Perhaps the threat is part of the attraction.

Over the years, both Mary and I had grown more than blasé about Niagara Falls ourselves; the thrill had diminished, and our driving tour was unusual for the fact that we were making it voluntarily, not at the behest of visiting friends or relatives. We'd done the pilgrimage to the roaring plunge often enough for the signs along The Parkway to seem a bit coy. The Gorge. The Whirlpool. We get it, already: this isn't just any canyon or big eddy, and these are not no-name Falls. *We know where we are.* The word omitted from the signs is the one that doesn't have to be said here. "Niagara" is understood, grammatically at least. The word itself is trickier than the signs would have you believe, and the place itself may be trickier still. "Niagara" is an Iroquoian or Algonkian word with a meaning linguists haven't been able to decipher, except to say that it falls in the range of "many waters" or "thundering waters" or "liquid hell breaks loose over rock."

I must have been ready to be impressed again. Skirting the wild edge of The Gorge, we drew closer to The Falls. From the abandoned bottle caps, pop-tabs and flattened cigarette packages that dotted one of the scarifying grassy ledges between the road and the seventy-metre drop, it was obvious that certain ceremonies had been conducted. Spiritual thrillseekers of a different kind. We passed Thomas Barnett's Niagara Falls Museum, repository of his personal collection of oddities: a must-see for more than a century. We passed under a more recent attraction, the casino. Then we saw The Mist; we heard The Noise. Other distractions aside, The Monumentality of it all was becoming unavoidable. This was nature writ large and unambiguous, in its two basic components of rock and water.

As we drove under the last traffic light, I began to think that if a person really wanted to do something in response to what's happening here, if he was looking for a single, appropriate act to perform when close enough for it to seem necessary, he might fall on his knees. And apologize. Stupified awe, followed by immediate and abject sorrow in the face of anything that had ever been done to diminish this or any other place. In thought, word or deed. To every butterfly or stone, to every weed that ever emerged from a crack in the sidewalk.

There is no drive-by view of the cascade. We paid handsomely, parked, and approached on foot. Could we ever pay enough?

The falling-on-the-knees part is problematic. It places eye level below the top of a stone wall that guards the edge, so the object of awe and sorrow is out of sight. Socially, it could also be a bit dicey, though this is probably the one place on earth where the act seems natural. To ask The Question. Or ask again. Mary?

> I wish'd an hundred times that somebody had been with us, who could have describ'd the Wonders of this prodigious frightful Fall, so as to give the Reader a just and natural Idea of it, such as might satisfy him, and create in him an Admiration of this Prodigy of Nature as great as it deserves.

So wrote Father Louis Hennepin, a Jesuit priest who was among the first Europeans to see Niagara. I take comfort in not being the first to lament feeling at such a loss to give adequate response to this place. Hennepin's attempt, however inadequate, earned him a blue shield on a pole, similar to McQuesten's cemmorative shield on Burlington Heights. The shield stands very close to the edge of the Falls. In winter, it is coated with an armour of ice.

> This wonderful Downfall is compounded of two great Cross-streams of Water, and two Falls, with an Isle sloping along the middle of it. The Waters which fall from this vast height, do foam and boil after the most hideous manner imaginable, making an outrageous Noise, more terrible than that of Thunder; for when the Wind blows from off the South, their dismal roaring may be heard above fifteen Leagues off.

South is upriver, so Father Hennepin is talking about a wind that carried the sound through the canyon of the Gorge, over the fruitful lowlands and into the faces of the seventeenth-century tour and exploration group, of which he was a member, as the party paddled their canoes toward the escarpment face and the inevitable portage at Queenston. For water travellers, the louder the Roar the greater the Downfall, and the more Dismal the portage.

Reaching Niagara Falls itself, Hennepin was duly overwhelmed. He passed through the area both coming and going in his travels and wrote about it twice in the same book, *A New Discovery of a Vast Country in America*. The book provided a travelogue for armchair tourists who would never journey to that vast country, and became a bestseller when it was published in 1698.

> The Waters tumble down together into the Gulph, with all the violence that can be imagin'd, from a Fall of six hundred Foot, which makes the most Beautiful, and at the same time most Frightful Cascade in the World ... When one stands near the Fall, and looks down into this most dreadful Gulph, one is seized with Horror, and the Head turns round, so that one cannot look long or stedfastly upon it.

Three hundred years and however many millions of onlookers later, one still does not look long or steadfastly upon it, but the reasons have perhaps changed. People come, walk, gaze, snap a few shots or switch on the camcorder, stand around and turn away after a remarkably brief period of time. They sit on the stone rail with their backs to the Falls. Niagara is a one-act show after all, and in more than one way has lost the extreme edge it had when Hennepin first came and heard and saw.

The nineteenth century was already trying to raise the excitement level, to involve human beings in the natural drama, with tightrope artists who performed various stunts while crossing the gorge. Then the turbines were installed, and drew away the power of the river itself. I used to think it was magic, that behind the curtain of the Falls, hydro-electric power was invisibly being produced. In reality, upstream channels on both sides divert water from the river into huge reservoirs which, at their generating end farther downstream, take advantage of the seventy-metre drop of the escarpment to drive the turbines, which then discharge the water back into the river from behind massive concrete walls. As much as one third of the flow of the Niagara River is diverted into the channels, meaning that the river's velocity is nowhere near what Hennepin witnessed.

The land around the Falls has been tamed as well. The dangerous, overhanging rock has been blasted away. The massive and messy pile of rocks at the base of the Falls has been removed. The surroundings are graced with parkland and other passive attractions. Niagara has lost much of its sublime appeal during our two hundred years of settlement. The Spiritual Horror—for that's what I think Hennepin experienced—that the Falls inspired, its liquid violence over rock, is considerably diminished today. Hennepin's more than doubling of the height of the Falls, in error or for effect, now seems quaint. At the same time, the power of the place has taken on an entirely different, sinister form. You can hardly *not* think about the invisible dripping of toxic leakage through the walls of the Gorge from the waste sites above when you are standing there, innocently attending a natural wonder.

THE AREA AROUND Niagara Falls first started to be settled one hundred years after Father Hennepin's visit, when American citizens loyal to the British crown were forced from their homes during the Revolutionary War. Many of these refugees were funnelled through the narrow gap between the two lakes, Erie and Ontario, crossing the Niagara River into territory that the British controlled, where they were granted five-hundred-acre parcels of land. This is when, for instance, Richard Beasley came to Head of the Lake.

Not many years after that first influx, an advertising campaign made it widely known in the United States that land was available in this area, and practically free for the claiming. The same Lieutenant-Governor John Graves Simcoe who visited the Beasleys for dinner hoped to bulk up the population, to help withstand the attack from the south he thought was inevitable. As a result, even greater numbers made the journey north. Niagara was in the news, so to speak, because so many folks were travelling past it. Soon, tourists began arriving.

From the start, newlywed couples were attracted to the Beauty and the Terror, following the example of the honeymooning daughter and son-in-law of the President of the United States, who made the trip in 1801. It has been so ever since. They come to stand on the Edge, to stare in stunned contemplation at the sheer immensity of what they have undertaken. They experience a non-rational, glad hankering to let their jaws drop while peering into the dreadful Gulph of the unknown that lies before them, to let nature slap them in the face. It's the big metaphor they're after—the poetry. After a few minutes they turn from the Frightful Cascade, and go pick up the key to a theme suite. They may as well attempt to unite rock and water as to unite their bodies and souls, but that is what they will endeavour to do. Their aim, their pleasure, their promise. The impossible.

For as long as the sun shall rise, the wind blow, and the water fall—or as long as they can generate the energy. The Falls slowly recedes into the background, where it will remain over the course of however many years the couple stays together, a white background hum that may occasionally swell into the Terrible Noise that threatens to overwhelm them.

Niagara confirms the monumentality of what any human pair does, making history, while it also provides immeasurable comfort in the knowledge the newly-attached are but two small brush strokes on the edge of a great landscape.

THE WATER AND ROCK have been making history, too.

When Niagara first plunged over the edge of the escarpment, the water fell directly into glacial Lake Iroquois. There it joined the clockwise current common to large bodies of water in the northern hemisphere, and travelled west along the base of the escarpment. This west-flowing current met the east-flowing waters descending through the Dundas Valley, and created the Iroquois Bar.

The waters flowed because the glaciers were melting. Ice still blocked the valley of the Saint Lawrence River, which today drains Lake Ontario into the Atlantic. Lake Iroquois, which was Lake Ontario's predecessor, reached the ocean through the Mohawk and Hudson Valleys, where New York City is now.

When the ice block melted, the level of Lake Iroquois quickly fell as the water slipped out the side door of the Saint Lawrence Valley. It was during this geographical rush hour that the ravines in the lake's raised shoreline were carved, and the building of the Bar halted. The Bar became a finished work—as finished as any physical feature of the landscape can be in this story. As the waters receded, the Bar was revealed, emerging into full view, high and dry, lying where no wave or current could reach or shape it, for now. For that's the thing about the landscape: it looks so permanent and stable, yet it's all so tentative, a work-in-progress.

This event—the melting of the ice block in the Saint

Lawrence—was Day One for Niagara Falls as we know it from our honeymoons and visits with relatives from overseas.

At first, the drop in the water level of Lake Iroquois meant only a longer drop for the water falling over the lip of the escarpment into the new, shallower lake. In fact, the water now fell the full height of the escarpment. But the escarpment has a weak foundation: the rock at its base is softer than on its top. With the softer rock exposed, the water began to dig in, eroding and undermining the foundation until the harder rock at the top was cantilevered like a balcony over the cavity it had hollowed out below. When the balcony could no longer bear its own weight, it collapsed, and another bite was taken out of the escarpment.

It's been twelve and a half thousand years since the ice dam melted, and in that time the Falls has chewed its river channel, the Niagara Gorge, through approximately eleven kilometres of rock. It is now halfway to its source, Lake Erie. It is also three hundred metres upstream from where Father Hennepin stood. The process has been slowed since the advent of hydro-electric generation, when the Niagara River was partially diverted and its flow became regulated, but if twelve and a half thousand years is only a few minutes on the terrestrial clock, then these current impositions amount to mere seconds of delay.

I STAND AT THE FALLS with my companion of many years and think *young, young, young,* each time now that we make the trip. It *is* a revelation how truly youthful, in the grand scheme of things, Niagara is. At the same time, those two have been going for ages, the water and the rock. And they're still at it.

As though they had from now until forever, the two opposites are still making an Impossible Beauty.

And you can get here from there. You can get to the Iroquois Bar from Niagara Falls. With your eyes closed. You can get here by following the edge of the Gorge from the falls to the face of the Niagara escarpment, at Queenston Heights. From there, it's a three-day trek along the escarpment edge, over a path that winds through the surprising wilderness of rock, waterfall, fruit farm and vineyard, city and suburb, that this two-hundred-year-old marriage between people and place has produced. This *second* marriage, since the original couple was split apart with the arrival of the first white settlers.

A rock cairn marks Kilometre 1 of the path, which is called the Bruce Trail. The Bruce Trail travels through Hamilton on its seven-hundred-and-eighty-two kilometre journey north to the tip of the Bruce Peninsula, and it passes the spot where the Iroquois Bar and the escarpment meet. Where, you can stand on the edge overlooking the city and wonder at the relationship these many years on, this late in the marriage game; at the difficulties involved, the mutual accomodations; at how to repair long-term hurts and still enjoy the companionship. How to keep the edge, person to person, and person to place, where respect and concern for the welfare of one with whom you are in daily physical contact stand in sharp relief against the horizon, balanced against the sheer drop.

# The Jump

"I was right beside him when he jumped."

"Pardon me?"

"I was standing right beside Chic during the big dance when he climbed the rail and jumped into the canal."

The woman on the other end of the line (I was on the phone again) was named Bernadette (not the same Bernadette as my ravine-walking companion). She was in her late seventies and had grown up in one of the boathouses beside the Desjardins canal. "Boathouse" is a broad term. Some of them were two-storey structures with living quarters above and garage-like boat storage below, while others were single-storey houses the size of a small cottage. Some were well-constructed, others slapped together. Collectively, the assemblage of dwellings was also known as Shantytown, or Shacktown.

"Ours wasn't a shack at all. It was a real house. Most of them were."

The dance Bernadette was referring to took place June 15, 1932, when the disassembling of the community was well underway. Some of the houses were being taken apart and salvaged for lumber, others bulldozed into oblivion, and

others, like Bernadette's, were sold whole and moved. The Easterbrook family lived farther up the north shore of the bay and had opened a restaurant there. They also ran a small resort below the restaurant, at a beach on Willow Cove. Three of the doomed boathouses were purchased by them and relocated during the winter with a team of horses that pulled the homes across the ice to the beach, where they became summer cottages.

Bernadette had been telling me about a childhood on the opposite side of Iroquois Bar from the Mercers and Bruntons, at the bay end of the short Desjardins canal. She talked about the coal that fell from the trains which passed almost directly over their roof, useable lumps, that she and her sister were sent to collect; the one-pound bricks of butter the entire community gathered and spirited into their iceboxes, "to save the butter from spoiling," after a railway mishap; the sparks from trains that set houses ablaze, including their next door neighbour's, an event which sent her own family to live in the motel directly above, on York Boulevard, while their house was repaired of smoke damage.

The dog who rescued a small girl who had fallen through the ice.

The neighbour who rowed his pregnant wife, in labour, across the bay; the couple's two-kilometre walk to the hospital, where the wife gave birth; their return, later the same day, in the same boat, during a storm, with the baby.

*Iroquois Bar, from Carroll's Point*

Bernadette had not one but two memories equivalent to George Mercer's spring of "coolest, clearest, sweetest-tasting water." A fruit tree near their home had blossomed twice the same year, and Chic Collura had jumped from the High Level Bridge into the canal.

"He did it on a bet. Ten dollars. I know he did because I was standing right there. I was ten years old."

It was the evening before the day of the grand opening ceremony for the bridge. At the ceremony all the notables would be in official attendance. The evening celebration, however, was for the people. York Boulevard had been closed, cars were parked on the grass, and a dance, with full orchestra, was taking place on the bridge itself. Members of the boathouse community—those who hadn't yet been displaced—climbed up to join the festivities.

"I watched him climb onto the rail, and before anyone could stop him, down he went."

His flight was as brief an episode in the life of the evening as the two generations of people who lived beside the Desjardins canal were themselves only a brief moment's dreaming in the whole long night of the Iroquois Bar. Thirty metres. One hundred feet.

But it's all slow motion in the eyes of the ten-year-old on the bridge, on the other end of the phone line, and Chic falls one layer at a time, through the eons of water-carried, wave-laid sand and gravel, pebble and cobble; falls feet first, through beaches formed by generational millennia of ice age lapping and crashing. All time and place is contained in this outlandish, delicious act of plunging slowly, one single scoop at a time, of following the shovels as they dig a path through the air, eighty years earlier, for the man descending past what the shovels nudge and uncover, then slipping into, entering the canal.

"He hit the water and we saw him come up and swim to shore. A couple of his friends helped him out and he laid down on the sand for a while. Winded. Then they helped him up and got away along the tracks before the police came."

Chic had a reputation for stunts, is said to have jumped off more than one bridge.

Next morning, the ribbon-cutting. Thomas B. McQuesten is in attendance. As usual, he makes himself as inconspicuous as possible for the photographs. Cars begin to flow across. There is a knock on the door of Chic's home not far away, on Hess Street. Storylines and contour lines cross, criss-cross: Hess runs down into the old, closed inlet and intersects Barton Street.

It's the police. Chic's father answers the door and tells them Chic's not in, he's at work.

"He never got caught," said Bernadette. "I don't know if he collected on the bet, though. You'll have to ask someone else."

And that's that. Wild dance hero one evening, the next morning back on the shop floor.

# The whole night going on without us

Only the scale is different. The same elements of water and land that worked together to make the different beach-scapes that my brother and I woke to each morning of summer vacation also made this landscape where I live. The body of land is bigger, and the time taken by the water, sand and stones a much longer span of hours than a single summer night, but the effect, too, is the same.

The Creation story in the book of Genesis makes sense to me when it describes the seventh day as one of rest. The story always seemed to me to be based on observation and a felt experience of the world. The world looks and feels like a finished work. It's apparent that a lot of time and effort has gone into the lay of the land, the general construction and shape of things; into the diversity of animal life, plants, insects; the sun, the sea, the sky; all things bright and beautiful. It's just as apparent, to the naked eye, that the job is done.

There's no guarantee, of course, that tomorrow we won't be driven from home by rising waters or plunging temperatures and another impossibly cold wall or blanket of ice (or the opposite, in this age of global warming), but after twelve-

and-a-half-thousand years there has been a long enough lull between the elements' working nights for everyone to have settled comfortably into the landscape, to have built up a reserve of confidence that the physical world will stay more or less as it is. To keep playing on the beach as if this Sunday vacation will never end.

The scale of this sandbar is part of its attraction for me, as though my childhood experience of the beach landscape has been given size and substance. The landscape that I loved has grown up around me, enlarged to proportions only slightly less than mythic. I live within these grand proportions, only slightly larger now than I was then. It seems a gift, rather than an insult or challenge, to be physically humbled in this way, a kindness, and just plain luck that by choice and circumstance I should be living in a place where I feel understood within the landscape. Where I don't have to explain myself.

Is it a peculiarity of immigrants, or of the children of immigrants, that they feel the need to explain their presence? Or, in one form or another is it a question that everyone asks themself, or that the earth asks of us? *Explain yourselves.*

As the landscape continues to explain itself, as it slowly reveals more of its story, it remains a source of wonder to me how much of that story is written by water. Water in all forms, frozen and free, as hard as rock or running through the fingers. Water coming and going in successive waves that shove and shape and reshape the earth beneath them into hills and valleys, and leave behind snaking piles of stones and rocks, or huge boulders that stand singly, inexplicably, in farmer's fields, *erratics*, that must be ploughed around. Water that fills large inland lakes covering greater and different areas than this lake we live beside, creating raised shorelines and beaches. Water in currents, in torrents, carving ravines through red shale, gorges through the rock wall of the escarpment, sculpting. Waterwork on top of waterwork on top of waterwork. And always the same water, in the same cycle of evaporation, condensation, precipitation, the same water flowing through Eden, through the ravine Bernadette and I walked one spring day, through the culvert into the bay.

If the earth's story is water, so is our own. Our clay could not be shaped, dry.

The Iroquois Bar and the glaciated landscape that surrounds it have a hands-on feel. Water is the hand, a hand intimate with the visible world, and the sensuality of its continual liquid play over these shapes, over time, presents a pure and unabashed eroticism. Endless hours of touch. Love on the long afternoon of the seventh day.

WITH ALL THIS WATER TALK I can't help also wondering if something tribal isn't going on with this immigrant son. A racial memory that I am part of, that's part of me, and a whole long night going on in generations of that other, water-worked land, the Netherlands, connecting where I come from to where I am.

It was my father who first introduced my brother and me to the pleasures of building dams. Our Sunday afternoon family walks along the North Saskatchewan River were punctuated by long interludes of piling up rocks and stones and pieces of wood across the streams that joined it. This often seemed the point of the walk, at least for my brother and me. My father squatting, gathering double handfuls of stones and tossing them into the stream, we his helpers. Three boys, playing with water.

Frequently other Sunday walkers would stop to watch, but no one ever offered or asked to join us, and we had the sense that ours was an unusual activity. More than once a man out with his own family stopped and stood beside my stooped father and said, "I wish I could still do that." As if whatever prevented him was strong enough to constitute a physical restraint. What's stopping him? I wondered. My father himself felt no such restraint; why would anyone else? We'd finish the dam, then Dad would get up and continue walking, leaving us to decide where to poke the hole that would release the water again, before we ran to catch up.

We later moved east and began vacationing beside Lake Huron. The flat, sandy beach of that inland sea created a different relationship between streams and the bigger water the streams entered than did the steeper slopes of the North Saskatchewan River. There was more give and take in the conversation. The lake appeared the more powerful, but in the world of water the smallest pool or stream can have a voice forceful as a flood, as anyone with the merest trickle of a household plumbing problem knows. My father had grown up in a country where the conversation between water and water, between water and land and people, was part of the national dialogue, and maybe also a part of the inner dialogue of the people themselves.

The town where my father was born, in the northern section of the Netherlands, is, as the name of the country suggests, below sea level. Not all of the country is below sea level, but the people who live in what is now the province of Friesland have been contending with water ever since they settled there—water raining from above, attacking horizontally as it stormed in over the North Sea—or water invading as the ground force of the sea itself, leaving them scrambling to stay high and dry. When the Roman Empire came calling, Roman writers commented on the marsh-like conditions, and wondered why anyone would choose to stay. The place hardly looked worth the effort of living there, much less of conquering.

The Frisians protected themselves against regular flooding by the North Sea by scooping up earth into mounds. When the North Sea invaded, they gathered their animals, retreated to the top of the mounds, and waited. More than a thousand of these diminutive hills dotted the lowland when the Romans first arrived.

They waited while the sea swirled around their handiwork, and watched as it deposited silt at the base of each hill. By building ring dikes around the silt, with one-way valves that allowed the water to leave but prevented its re-entering, the Frisians gradually increased the size of their hills. Though the shapes described by these property lines of piled soil were still fluid, constantly shifting between the claims of the people and the claims of the sea, the hills eventually grew wide enough to accomodate farmhouse and barn, and over the centuries whole towns grew up around them. It is possible to drive over the flat farmland of the province today and be simultaneously in view of four or five towns, each one bumped-up slightly on the horizon and identifiable by its steeple, which rises even higher over the roofs than it otherwise might because the church is standing on the crest of the *terp*, as these small hills are called.

Someone nearer to the source of my generational stream must have been closely enough related to these human-crafted features of the landscape to be named after them, but my surname, Terpstra, is really the only connection I have now to a life surrounded by the sea and threatened with regular flooding. The name, plus whatever characteristics of body and behaviour can be attributed to a person of northern European stock, or to a distinct race like the Frisians. It wasn't until my parents took Mary and me on a trip to the Netherlands thirty years after their emigration that I saw the country for the first time.

During that trip, we stopped one day in Harlingen, an old Frisian port on the coast of the North Sea. It was market day and the town was full of people. Mary and I walked together through the streets, among the crowds, but within ten or fifteen minutes we both were experiencing an odd feeling of uneasiness. We couldn't pin down the cause of this feeling immediately, but then realized, to our surprise, that it came from our surroundings, the place itself, the people. Almost everyone looked fair-haired, fair-skinned, and stood consistently a little taller than the norm. In other words, they looked like us. Rather, we looked like them.

Mary and I both were born on the New World side of the big water, and we've lived in various North American cities and suburbs. The people we've moved among on the streets of home have always come in a variety of shapes, sizes and shades. In the Dutch communities in North America where we were raised, we experienced a similar if more limited physical diversity, because even a small country like the Netherlands produces, over the centuries, people of different, so to speak, model types.

There, in Harlingen, for the first time in our lives, we found ourselves walking among those of our own racial stock, our ethnic kin, which until that moment we did not fully realize existed—existed so identifiably and powerfully that it would stop us in our tracks, and make us feel so strangely out of place. This was where our bodies came from, where the clay and water were originally mixed together and shaped. It was as though we'd been turned upside down and for the first time had a good look at our labels: *Made in Friesland.*

A person's sense of uniqueness can take a hit in those circumstances. Mine suffered a second blow. Our shared surname is fairly unusual on this side of the Atlantic, but in Friesland it was common as mud. We took a photograph of me leaning against a storefront farther up the street, beneath a sign:

TERPSTRA

FURNITURE

I'd just started making furniture as a livelihood at the time, unwittingly following another instinctual path, I suppose, and there it was, succinct and declarative: who I am, what I do.

HARLINGEN SITS BEHIND the ring dike that now protects the entire coastline of Friesland. The dike and canal system is a later approach to the flooding problem than the terp, and has made the terps by and large redundant. The system has proved pretty durable, too, though the idea didn't spring from the Frisians or the Dutch, but from the Romans. The Romans figured that if they were going to live in the area as conquerors, as their own instinctual path dictated they should, the environment would have to be altered, and made more accommodating. The Empire required communication and trade routes, the easy flow of traffic, soldiers. Travel is difficult when roads flood. The first dikes protected the ways in and out, the defensive act of an invader against liquid guerilla activity.

The locals embraced and expanded on the idea after the Romans left, and in the sixteenth century the Dutch went on the offensive. Prompted by population pressure in the province of Holland, south of Friesland, they began pumping water out of places they had never lived before. One man, Adriaan Leegwater (*leeg*, in Dutch, means "empty" or "to empty"), had the idea of draining a large inland lake, the Beemer Zee. With a double ring of dikes around the lake and a battalion of windmills to pump the water up and into canals that drained into the North Sea, and against a battalion of naysayers, he eventually succeeded. It kicked off an industry, with lake after lake becoming *polders* (reclaimed lowland) over the next two hundred years.

By the twentieth century, the Dutch were still at it, on a monumental scale. The *Afsluitdike* (shut-off dike) was completed in 1932, and it represented a kind of imperialism over the sea that would do the Romans and Adriaan Leegwater proud. The storied Zuyder Zee, or Southern Sea, was effectively separated from the North Sea by this thirty-two-kilometre bar of earth, reed and concrete, and demoted to lake status. *Zee* became *meer* (lake), and was re-named for the river that flows into it, the Ijssel. The former sea was divided into four large polders, each to be defined by its own ring dike, with sea lanes between. One of the polders was diked and drained immediately following the completion of the main dike. Another had its dike in place but was not yet drained when we visited, because competing interests in the country coveted its acreage. By this time, too, some Dutch people were going against the national grain and questioning the very idea of reclaiming land from the sea.

We drove across a third polder, imagining the sunken ships and Second World War planes that had slowly been revealed lying in their resting places on the sea bottom when the area had been drained. It takes a few years for the earth to make the transition from sea bed to arable land. Rapeseed waved in the new fields, drawing salt out of the soil. The countryside of the Zuyder Zee polder lay flat as Canadian prairie. That bump on the horizon we were driving toward, my parents told us, was Urk, an island, now landlocked—a defunct island, a terp of a different order. During their long isolation in the middle of the *zee*, the residents of Urk had developed their own habits of dress, speech and culture, and had also maintained older habits that had vanished from the general Dutch world—a world from which they were no longer protected, and that now threatened them with a different order of flood.

You can see what Erasmus meant. It was he, I believe, who coined a saying to the effect that God created the world, while the Dutch made the Netherlands. My people strain against entering that seventh day of rest. Plans exist to link the series of islands off the Frisian coast with dikes, and to drain the Waddenzee, which separates the islands from the shore. As a child, my mother vacationed on one of those islands, Ameland. My Dutch cousins, and hosts of other citizens, have actively fought against the plan.

We saw another example of ongoing creative activity in the landscape of my parents' youth when we went to visit the farm where my father's maternal grandparents lived, and where he had spent summers as a child. Their farm was situated on the coastline, snugly set beside the sinuous, green snake of a dike that rimmed the countryside. From its top my father used to watch the fishing boats on the Lauwer Zee, a large bay of the North Sea. Between then and the time of our visit, another dike had been built, across the mouth of the bay. The water had been pumped out, and the view from the top of the earlier dike was of farms and fields stretching to a dry horizon.

Dad showed us the stall in the barn where he'd slept. He showed us the narrow canal, a ditch, that he'd pole-vaulted across in the time-honoured Dutch child's game, in which the runner charges at the canal, stabs his pole into the middle of the water, and hopes the momentum will vault him to the opposite side. He told us about the time he made it only halfway across and stopped, stranded, a small boy clinging to a pole, rehearsing explanations for his grandmother as he began sliding down into the muddy water.

He also showed us the barn doorway, the beam that he had failed to notice as a child, until it knocked him off the top of a hay wagon pulled by his grandfather's horse. He had broken his wrist in the fall, a break that would bother him, off and on, the rest of his life. We were leaving the barn as he told this story, the three of us listening, ducking beneath a heavy wooden beam that barred the wide doorway at chest height. Following us, Dad came up too soon and did it again: brained himself on a beam, fifty years later.

How much of a people's character is determined by the conditions their natural environment places on them? How much that is Dutch in character comes from living under the threat of liquid invasion, the water wanting the land back again?

The Dutch may now never enter the seventh day. The reclaimed lake and sea bottoms require constant pumping to keep the water out. The dike-line of defense is continually under assault from the sea and requires constant attention over every square inch to make sure that the water hasn't begun to find or wear a way in, or around, or under—because water does, and will. A dike, even one that is hundreds of years old, that has been subsumed into the landscape and lies hidden and forgotten, can remain essential, its breach, catastrophic. When my sister lived in Amsterdam one year, underground digging for sewers or a subway cut through one of these forgotten dikes, flooding the basements for a wide area of the city. The Dutch can't stop paying close attention to where they live, nor drop their guard. One's first obligation is to the dike; water-defense responsibilities of the Dutch citizen, by law, supercede all others.

You might forgive a person, and forgive a people, if under these circumstances, over the centuries, they become a bit obsessive over details, over putting everything in its proper place, over the one, right way of doing things—which happens to coincide with their own, together with the one right way of thinking, which also happens to coincide with their own. Doing things their way ultimately is the only guarantee of a dry life, but also of an afterlife, because having themselves created, as Erasmus said, the Netherlands, they have likewise been given the keys to that landscape at the highest elevation, which is to say, heaven. Or so it seemed my ethnoreligious upbringing was leading me to believe.

First-hand knowledge of the unleashed strength of the sea can instill a native humility, while imposing and maintaining imperialist claims on the sea might encourage a native pride.

You don't want to be accepting applause while standing on a dike if the sea is your audience, but how can these people not know what they have accomplished, and accomplish daily: their works are ever before them.

My father did not mind that the joke was on him when he slid down the pole into the ditch, or was knocked off the hay wagon as a child. His second braining was one for the books, though. I relish the memory, not out of any latent hostility toward him on my part (his head is also my head), but because, when placed beside certain characteristics already mentioned, including a stubborn, clay-like impermeability to new ideas, a conviction that one basks in divine light (a notion the Dutch are not necessarily alone in entertaining), such pratfall is antidote. It seems purposeful. Particularly when delivered from above.

TWO YEARS AFTER my parents emigrated, the Netherlands experienced a flood. It happened in the southern part of the country, the delta of the Rhine River. The delta is a maze of larger and smaller channels flowing between many islands. Each of the islands are protected by its own ring dike, but on the night of February 1, 1953 nothing could prevent the combination of upstream runoff and a storm from the North Sea from breaking through. By the time the storm cleared, eighteen hundred and thirty-five people had drowned, fifty thousand farm animals were lost; forty-seven thousand homes and one hundred and thirty-three villages and towns were under water. Close to half a million acres of land were lost.

I grew up with two books that depicted the Netherlands and the sea, books that helped to shape my sense and feeling of what living in the old country meant. One was called simply *de ramp*. The flood. Its cover was entirely filled by a single, black-and-white photograph of a horse standing in water. Nearby stood a cow. Both were nearly up to their bellies in water. The tufts of a few bushes showed above the low waves. The photo continued around the spine to the back cover, which showed a road sign and the guardrails of a short bridge, also half-immersed. On the endpapers, the photograph was reproduced, but in reverse, as if its pictorial truth lay in the fact that the same scene could be repeated backwards and forwards, because the water was coming and going from all directions.

For a child, the scene was incongruous and fascinating. Water was ubiquitous, with the normal fixtures of everyday life, inanimate and animate, sticking up through it. It seemed almost impossible to me that one or two feet of water could make such a difference over so great an area. But it was a condition of their landscape that the Dutch—of whom I seemed to be one—lived with.

Inside were more photos, and a text of which I could make out only snatches. The black-and-white photographs, including the one on the cover, were really more light brown and beige. Brown and beige paper and photographs were associated in my mind with the Second World War, and with shortages, and so to me the country of my parents' origin and upbringing came to mean war, deprivation and flood.

Water foamed past shop windows in the middle of the night, as the sea swept in through breaches in the dikes. Farmers and their families waved signal flags from the roofs of their homes. The photos showed the disaster, the fight and the recovery, and everyone pitching in. Soldiers handed babies up to men in fishing boats, people hoisted sandbags that had been filled by schoolchildren with shovels. Queen Juliana toured the area, giving moral support and encouragement. Loaves of bread were piled up under the pipes of the church organ. One photo showed a shoreline on which domestic debris had washed up and collected. Standing on top of the long heap was a child's rocking horse.

The book made a deep impression on me. The flood was a natural catastrophe, but already I had the sense that nature was not solely responsible.

The second book was called *The Delta Works*. The photos were colour and the text English. In response to the Flood of '53, the ring dikes around the islands were being rebuilt, and a new dike system constructed, island to island, across the mouth of the delta. The Rhine would flow into the North Sea through a series of sluice gates which allowed the water out but could shut like valves to keep the sea from entering, an adaptation of the system that had first been used to contain the reclaimed silt around the terps. Here, though, the gates would be regulating the flow of tidal waters.

The book itself was small, but that only served to emphasize the staggering scale of the project. The Delta Works project carried the *never again* quality of statements made after the war, a quality reinforced by the fact that the project would be finished only in the distant future. It seemed heroic and hopeless. The ships dropping their loads of fill into the sea and the cranes dangling their caissons in the air appeared much too tiny to ever finish the task.

The Delta Works was completed in the 1980s, but the threat never goes away. When one threat is dealt with, another may appear. Water conditions change as climate conditions change. In recent years some flooding has taken place in the Rhine delta due to swollen river levels deeper in Europe. Portions of reclaimed land have tactfully been returned to the sea in a kind of pre-emptive peace offering in the face of rising water levels all over the world. The Dutch are always responding to the life-and-death matter of their own landscape.

IT'S ALWAYS A MATTER of life and death. If sea levels fell instead of rising, and dikes became as redundant as terps, if peoples migrated, and a new tribe entered the (former) Netherlands, these new settlers would wonder at the elongated humps of earth that stretched to the horizon, and would invent stories of how the odd little tumuli that dotted the landscape came to be. The stories would likely revolve around questions of spirit. My Frisian forebears built those tumuli to save their souls. The terps became the sites of barn-like buildings where the people gathered every week to listen and sing and pray. To which they routinely fled, in fear, gratitude, hope and grief, belief and superstition. Around the holy Sunday barns lay burial grounds, around which grew towns. Only matters of life and death explain people and their most simple creations.

I stand on top of, or beside, the sand-and-gravel bar here in my home and native land, on this side of the ocean, and it looks to me like nothing so much as the dike beside my great-grandparents' farm by the Lauwer Zee. Am I attracted to this glacial artifact because of something that flows through the canals of my veins? Were Mary and I attracted to each other for similar reasons?

A sense of place and belonging is a matter of blood, circumstance and choice. The day we climbed to the top of the dike beside my great-grandparents' farm I was relatively new to the city, Hamilton, that sits on the bed of what once was Lake Iroquois, on land reclaimed, as it were, from a glacial sea. I was as yet unaware of the Iroquois Bar as a land feature, much less as a creation of water. Now, when I recall climbing the dike my father climbed as a child to see boats and the sea, I feel as though I was being remembered. It was not, however, the diked and drained land of my forebears calling and recalling me to myself, but this one. I felt myself a part of this landscape for the first time there, in that foreign landscape of my father's childhood.

# *Lay-by*

P/15 MIN     (5:03–5:18 P.M.)

5:03–5:08     103 VEHICLES PASS BY.

One end of the imaginary line that crosses the road ties me to a stone on a terp-like hill, a stone which remembers immigrants and soldiers to this landscape. The other end ties me to a blue shield that commemorates the work of one who stuck his finger in the civic dike, to save this landscape from other, non-liquid kinds of inundation.

5:08     TWO FISHERS, WITH POLES, WALKING BAY SIDE TOWARD END OF BAR; ONE BLUE CAR, PARKED OPPOSITE; MAN, WOMAN, TWO KIDS, EXPLORING CHOLERA STONE.

I come to remember who I am, and where.
    Through the leafless trees the bay is visible on one side, the marsh on the other.

| | |
|---|---|
| 5:09 | GREEN VAN PULLS IN BEHIND ME; DRIVER, MALE, STAYS INSIDE. |
| 5:10 | SPORTY RED CAR, ACROSS; YOUNG MALE EMERGES, SITS ON MCQUESTEN STAIRS, SMOKES. |

I come to save myself from the floods of forgetfulness; to keep from being carried off and drowned by the rush-away sound of traffic here and below; to watch and wait for the waters to recede so I can go home, return to the routines of living.

| | |
|---|---|
| 5:11 | GREY CAR PARKS IN FRONT; TWO FEMALES, ONE WITH BACKPACK, WALKING BAY SIDE TO BAR-END. |
| 5:12 | GREY CAR LEAVES; VAN PULLS OUT FROM BEHIND, PASSENGER STARES AT ME. |
| 5:12 | BLACK JEEP PULLS IN BEHIND, LEAVES HEADLIGHTS ON; CYCLIST, MALE, SHOOTS BY, HEADING TOWARD CITY. |

But perhaps the remembering required of me by the conditions of life and landscape is integral to those routines. I've been here before, and the ritual is bound to repeat: I will gather and herd my meagre belongings to this place again.

| | |
|---|---|
| 5:14 | MALE JOGGER, MARSH SIDE, TOWARD CITY. |
| 5:15 | SEAGULL HOVERS OVER MCQUESTEN. |
| 5:17 | CYCLIST, BAY SIDEWALK, MALE, TWO $1 \times 6 \times 36"$ PLANKS ON HIS CARRIER, TOWARD BAR-END. |

5:18    FAMILY GETS IN BLUE CAR OPPOSITE,
        PULLS AWAY.

The water comes, the water goes, in all directions. Here, where the line connecting terp to terp, memory to memory, passes over four lanes of constant motion, the stories are told. The tension some days is palpable, difficult to bear, but where line crosses lanes the bow touches the tightened strings, and the song of the individual, communal spirit is played.

# Looking for the Sandbar

I WANTED TO SEE IF IT WAS VISIBLE. The half of the Iroquois Bar that stretches across water is a distinct feature of the landscape, but I wanted to know if the Bar's elongated hump was as obvious where it lay stretched across the city. If it made a solid wave that translated, for instance, into a ridge of rooflines riding a little higher than the rest.

There was a reason for my curiosity. The greatest natural wonder can grow humdrum over time, but the least significant land feature can do exactly the opposite, and grow so large in the mind that you're certain others can't help but see, and agree, once you point it out to them. Put to the test, however, the place may turn turtle, and recede under its shell of asphalt, urbanization. Standing empty handed in front of bewildered friends, I'd be forced to ask, *Is it just me?*

I wanted to know if you could get there from here. If you could travel from your own heightened consciousness of a feature of the landscape, to the less-than-Niagara subtlety of the feature itself, without a loss in that feature's *presence.*

So I went to the point of connection. I went to the natural concurrence of two land features, where the Iroquois Bar and the Niagara Escarpment meet. If the downtown Bar wasn't visible from there, I knew a path that led to the top of the escarpment, where the higher vantage might help bring the Bar into view. The path itself was another feature of the landscape that had grown significant in my mind, a concurrence of the natural and the human.

GEOGRAPHY RULES. The day was very Dutch: grey, damp and overcast. Bone-damp greyness is a ticket, however, into the atmosphere of this settlement's past. Liquid stone November brings back the mid-nineteenth century, when Head of the Lake first came to life as town and city. The same weather exudes from the basement walls of churches and homes built then. You can almost feel the water infiltrating through the lack of parging and weeping tiles, hear it dripping from the sides of the railway tunnel that opened into Thomas B. McQuesten's backyard, or see and hear it slipping through the cracks in the face of the escarpment. The escarpment provided the stone for many of the buildings, and you can drift back a century and a half simply by standing next to it, in the right weather. And I'm always in the market for anything that will return me to the time when people first stopped here, gazed about, and pitched their tents of wood and stone, pole and bark.

The lower half of the escarpment is not really a wall but rather the ruin of a wall, a sloping skirt of rubble and debris that has fallen from the cliff face: rocks worked free in the freeze-thaw cycle. The top of this slope and the top of the Bar are at the same elevation, halfway to the summit of the escarpment. It was at this spot, around the year 1806, that James Durand built a house.

A stone house. Enough timber was standing at the time to build a hundred houses, but stone signified that the man meant business, both literally and in the sense that he had definite ideas and plans for his own place, and permanence, in the world. His was the only stone house in an area that sported few houses at all. It featured a widow's walk, a wraparound porch, and tall french doors. Stately yet modest, to judge by later photographs. It was referred to locally, by the few locals there were, as a mansion. Within ten years Durand had sold it and moved on.

He named the residence Bellevue—not be confused with a house of the same name built fifty years later on the top edge of the escarpment, almost directly above his own, which was torn down in the year 2000—having chosen the location for the view of the glacial lake beachfront that spread out before its front porch, with the bay two kilometres straight ahead in the distance, the lake off to the right, the marsh to the left, and the escarpment, after its hairpin turn around Head of the Lake, laid across the left half the horizon—all of which was, indeed, *très belle*.

He chose the spot, too, because the road up the escarpment ran past it. In a time of few settlements, fewer roads and a lot of geography, that fact made life, and business, much easier. Geography rules. Early settlement roads followed native paths. The paths were ancient, and followed the landscape, keeping to ridges and higher ground wherever possible, looking for the quickest, most expeditious way to get from A to B, and finding the least strenuous ways up impediments like the escarpment. Unlike paths such as the Bruce Trail or the Appalachian Trail, they were designed not for recreation but transportation. Travellers were on foot by necessity, not choice, and needed no greater degree of difficulty than the walk itself presented.

The path beside which Durand placed his front door climbed the escarpment from this spot, already halfway up. It was less steep than a staircase, but steep enough to reach the top as swiftly as possible without the walker having to resort to climbing hand over foot. At the summit, they could pause for a drink of water at a small stream which dropped over the edge there, if they had a moment. As they paused they could also take in the view, which from that higher vantage was *plus belle*.

A clue that any current road might have its roots in an earlier, native culture of foot travel is in the weave and wander it performs against the surveyor's grid. In Hamilton, King Street is one such road. King runs parallel to the escarpment and the shoreline of the bay, crossing and double-crossing the grid layout as it goes. Its disregard for straightness is actually a very close reading of the landscape. It traces the line that water leaves in the sand when a wave retreats. The original native path followed the raised ridge of the beach of Lake Algonquin, the glacial lake that preceded Lake Iroquois. The ridge lies between the escarpment and the present lake, running from the Niagara River to Head of the Lake. Natives had walked this ridge for centuries, and the Loyalists followed the path upon crossing the Niagara. Eventually the path became King's Highway 8, renamed simply King Street in the towns and cities that sprang up along its route. Loyal we came, loyal we remain.

As they travelled up the Niagara peninsula from the river, the Loyalists met a fork in the path upon reaching Head of the Lake. The right fork climbed and headed off across the bay along the top of the Bar—after two hundred years of settlement, it still manages to cut a diagonal swath through the city as York Boulevard. The left fork turned and climbed the side of the Bar laterally, southward toward the escarpment, reaching the top of the Bar and the escarpment face at the same time, in a lovely little concurrence of natural and *human* geography. In this story, that concurrence almost rates its being called a sacred spot. (If pressed, I would say that the other end of the Bar, where Old Guelph Road touches water level at Mercer's Glen before climbing the marsh shore, is another such spot.) There, where the path met the escarpment and turned to begin climbing, James Durand built his house.

The path from the fork to the escarpment still exists, if one makes allowances for those same two hundred years. It's now a major city street, named John, five lanes wide. I first clued in to the path's existence while sitting on Durand's front porch—making further allowances, since neither porch nor house still stand. I was at a concurrence of visible and invisible worlds.

City maps show John Street running north-south between escarpment and bay in a perfectly straight line that matches all the others laid out by Augustus Jones, the original surveyor. But it isn't straight. Looking toward downtown, John curves slightly to the right. From his front porch James Durand would not have been able to see the fork at what is now the corner of King and John Streets unless he'd chopped all the trees growing around this curve, for they would have blocked his view. Today the intersection is hidden behind the buildings that have since grown where those trees once stood.

The city of Hamilton was born on that front porch, though it would be more accurate to say that the town was conceived at Bellevue, and born at the fork below. The town was conceived on a piece of paper that lay on a desk inside a room within the house that James Durand built.

The story behind this paper conception indirectly involves General Isaac Brock and the War of 1812—the war with the Americans that Lieutenant-Governor Simcoe had seen coming. General Brock passed through the area of Head of the Lake one evening in August, 1812, and stopped for dinner at the Durands'. He was on his way from Fort George on the Niagara River to the western extreme of Upper Canada, in a hurry, because General William Hull had recently crossed the Detroit River and entered the province. A thirty-two-year-old captain, George Hamilton, would be fighting with Brock in the battle at the Detroit River.

Captain Hamilton accompanied the General to dinner that evening at the Durands'. In my mind, at least, he did. Both also stayed the night, in my mind. The next morning the Captain awoke and stepped onto the front porch, stretched his arms, rubbed his eyes, and was instantly enamoured of the vista that spread before him. After breakfast he and the British commander mounted their horses and followed the path to the top of the escarpment, intent on Detroit. I see the backs of their horses as they climb and stop briefly at the top to let the horses water. Captain Hamilton takes in the view one last time, and thinks, *I want to live here.*

This little scenario may be *all* in my mind: the product of a sketchy memory of scattered readings, and a helping of desire. General Brock did come to dinner, but whether Hamilton was with him, whether both stayed the night, and whether Brock's route to engage Hull took him up the escarpment the next morning, are entirely less certain than is the recorded presence of George Hamilton, with Brock, at the taking of Fort Detroit.

Or whether Hamilton was enamoured of the place. I would like to think that he was. Within three years of that dinner, he had purchased and taken up residence in Durand's home, and it was on a piece of paper in his room in Bellevue that a townsite first came to be drawn up, a town that centred around the fork in the path of King Street.

The paper must have been one powerful piece of work, because a year later Hamilton's non-existent town was chosen over the established, nearby towns of Ancaster, Dundas and Waterdown to be the judicial seat for the new District of Gore. The district was being organized to cope with the influx of American settlers and immigrants after the war, and the decision meant, in effect, that Hamilton's site *would* be settled.

The three older towns had all developed around streams with waterfalls, and they were not pleased that a place which did not even exist, and that made no sense in terms of the focus of settlement life—the mills that the waterfalls powered— was chosen over them. In the two hundred years since that decision, all three towns have more or less become suburbs of Hamilton, and now lie within city limits. It isn't hard to imagine that some of the ill feeling between town and city, which at times erupts into outright animosity, has roots wrapped around the pure, hard stone of that memory.

George was only following in his father's footsteps. Robert Hamilton founded the town of Queenston, having settled by the Niagara River after being forced to abandon his property and home in the United States. He died in 1809, before the war began, but George's family was still living in his father's home on the Niagara when British troops accidentally burned it to the ground in the latter part of the war. An earlier, unsuccessful attack over the river by the Americans had resulted in the death of General Brock. Uncertainty as to how long the threat along the border would continue prompted George to seek safety for his family at Head of the Lake.

So there is a symmetry here: the father plants a town at one end of a native path, the son walks farther along the path and plants his own. Located at the downriver end of the native portage around Niagara Falls, however, Queenston was a natural place to set up a commercial enterprise and grow a settlement. Hamilton's planned townsite, on the other hand, had more to do with real estate speculation, plain and simple, and with the manipulation of strings of privilege. For Loyalists such as the Hamiltons, land was cheap, or free, and many of these immigrants came into their new country heavily connected and interconnected, politically, familially and commercially. They were able to accomplish much of what their hands set out to do, such as inventing towns that would be legislated into existence by the government of the day.

According to John Weaver, a city historian, Hamilton was the "first speculative townsite to evolve into a major Canadian city," though at the time it was not unusual for American investors to purchase large tracts from their government to develop as townsites and farmland, as more and more territory was taken and treatied away from the natives and opened up for settlement in New York, Ohio, and other states.

Our streets are named after his family and friends, the extended Hamilton family, the family and friends of fellow investors: John, Mary, Catherine, Rebecca, James. My own street is named after his grandmother on his mother's side. As for the town itself, the logical choice—given its situation next to Burlington Heights, beside Burlington Bay—would have been Burlington. Head of the Lake has a definite felicity. Oh George. Was it you? Your friends? Or is my sketchy, reading memory correct this time, and did the folk of the newly-invented town themselves insist that the success of your venture be marked by naming it after you?

In Upper Canada, towns and cities were named after places in Britain or countries in continental Europe. Chatham, Guelph, Waterloo, Berlin, London, Paris. Or they were lifted from the original inhabitants—Niagara, Mississauga, Toronto, Ontario—as a kind of verbal vestige of displacement, a token, a salve on the collective conscience of the displacers, like naming a suburban development after the "Forest Glen" it removes. The native names are indigenous, lovely to say aloud, but a bit fraudulent, since these places are certainly no longer alive with the tongues that gave and first spoke these names.

I could do it. I could talk myself into claiming there's a greater honesty in naming the place after the person who took first advantage.

I am enamoured of the fact that the origins of this city lie at the specific spot in the landscape where the Iroquois Bar and the Niagara Escarpment meet. I imagine Captain George Hamilton to have been enamoured, too. There's the rub. In my mind—which has been established as a dubious guide, I grant—if people love the scene in which they choose to play out their days, they will care for and defend it. For others, the features that stir the same affection may well become its selling point. How far does it seep into the soul of any place, that its landscape from Day One is seen in terms of real estate?

Bellevue was bought and sold several times more during the nineteenth and twentieth centuries, after the Hamiltons' residency, and remained standing until the early 1940s, when it no longer made economic sense for the then-owner to maintain it. The stone walls came down, and the property of our founding real estate giant was parcelled out in a more egalitarian distribution of landed wealth. It became the small survey of modest brick homes that stands there today.

I look to see if parts of the old place were incorporated as architectural details, as was done at another survey-estate downtown, where stone and iron railings from the demolished mansion became accents for the newly-built houses. That doesn't appear to be the case here. As with the apartment buildings on the Bar, the dwellings of the anonymous many replace the homes of the notable few. As usual, I stand conflicted.

I'VE COME TO SEE if the Bar is visible under the streets of downtown, but three-storey apartments, a parking garage and a hospital block the sightlines.

Turning to climb the path for a higher vantage, all the facts and stories, the thoughts and feelings I've gathered about this place, its actors and their accomplishments, what they left or did not leave behind, what existed here then, and what's here now, feel like an oversized bundle of deadfall that I hoist onto my back. The bundle snags on whatever tree or fence or car mirror I walk past, but I keep picking up sticks and stones, tossed and lost objects, as I go. And the bundle travels with amazing lightness. Something about walking, the physical connection with the ground, footstep by step, carries its own authority. The earth seems to give to the walker as much as it is forced to give to those who have power over it. It allows me to *possess* what others, like George Hamilton, have owned.

When my parents first moved our family here from Edmonton, we lived on top of the escarpment in a recently-completed suburban survey, where the streets were named for towns and cities in Florida: Sarasota, Miami, Tampa. Arriving, we knew three facts about Hamilton: that it was a steel-producing Great Lake port, had a famous Rock Garden, and also had a mountain. Reality bore out the first two. The third made us laugh, as it does most first-timers. We'd spent our summer vacations camping in the Rocky Mountains, and knew a mountain when we saw one. The one-hundred-metre-high Niagara Escarpment did not qualify.

We soon began calling it the Mountain too, if only as a matter of conformity. Much later, the reason behind the exaggeration began to dawn on me. For most of the settlement's life, the escarpment may just as well have been a mountain for all the trouble it caused. Roads climbed to the top, but they were few, narrow and steep, and were often undermined by erosion, washed out by weather or blocked by fallen rock. The roads were not seriously improved until between the two world wars, so for more than a century the city was forced to grow east-west, along the relatively narrow shelf between escarpment and bay. One upshot of this is that today a trip downtown from the suburbs, most of which are built on top of the escarpment, is a form of time-travel, in which you find yourself descending into a world of salmon-coloured brick, that is five decades or more older than the world you left above.

The escarpment presented a physical reality, a barrier, and calling it the Mountain raised that reality to the level of metaphor. It was, if you will, an act of poetry. Given what we already know, it may also have been an act of advertising: the poetically-enhanced description of a certain piece of property in which you might be interested ...

The original native path up the Mountain served well enough for traffic on foot and on horseback, but was too steep for horses pulling the carts and wagons of settlers and town dwellers. Its grade couldn't be made less steep because of the stream and waterfall at the top, so early on in settlement life the first alternative access road was constructed. Travellers could then choose the old route, or follow the gentler slope of the newer route, which swung around the opposite side of Bellevue and then turned to loop around behind it. Bellevue, very early on, became a traffic island.

No longer crucial, the old route remained virtually unimproved over two hundred years. What's left is now a paved and dirt laneway that follows an original native path, and is a miraculously preserved piece in the very old story of the concurrence, here, of natural and human geography.

On one side of the laneway, the treed slope drops off steeply into the backyards of the homes below, while the escarpment wall, by which you can get here from Niagara Falls with your eyes closed, rises on the other. Part of the retaining wall for that first new access road that went around Bellevue still stands, a length of dry stacked stone sandwiched beneath the concrete supports of a still more recent access. Path, road, highway: three generations of Mountain travel, one atop the other.

Close to the crest, the Bruce Trail joins the native path, and at Kilometre 113.7 of the Trail's Iroquoia section the two reach the top landing of a staircase.

This is it. As close as is humanly possible to where the General and his Captain may, or may not, have allowed their horses to water. From here, through the clearing made for the stairway, and with the leaves off the trees, I thought that I might make out the Bar beneath the city.

I must have been dreaming. Again. It was obvious already from the bottom of the path that the Bar is entirely subsumed into the urban landscape, the covering blanket of buildings and streets. The glacial handiwork is simply not pronounced enough to force itself through. Is too subtle a land feature. I've been pushing. What am I really looking for?

The body. Again. I'm *still* looking. I am looking for the body, undefiled. I would like to see what the glacial waters left behind when they left the area, the stoney landscape of their immediate departure. When giants roamed. I want to see it twelve thousand years on, when the steady, slow accumulation of humus has made a soft dark skin the trees can sink their roots into. A solid treescape, rolling along with the larger pronouncements of hill or rock, interrupted by streams and bodies of water. Uninhabited wilderness. Bears. Wolves. Rattlesnakes. Smoke rising. Canoes on the bay. Natives fishing—the Simcoes purchasing salmon. Inhabited wilderness. Curl of campfire and hearth; I want the body undefiled but lived upon, lived with. The habited landscape. What George Hamilton saw when he first thought to arrange this marriage of place and people. Clearings in the trees, rail fencing, farms, orchards. The small grouping of buildings at a fork in the path materializing into a town. I am looking to see the love and desire this landscape evokes made manifest in the landscape of the city.

All while leaning on a railing at the top of the James Street stairs.

Eventually, I realize that the Iroquois Bar *is*, in fact, visible. It's entirely observable and even unavoidable, though not from this vantage. From the ground. It lies down with us like the earthen vestige of a culture long gone. We ride its low wave every day, see it rising at the end of the street, coast over it, live upon and beside it. Walkers, joggers, cyclists feel their hearts beat, meeting it. The lesson of the autumn equinox said to keep both eyes open; lesson two says, keep both feet on the ground. Return to being here. This is home, a city, where the marriage is at its most intense, complicated. A matter of life and death, not scenery.

WRITERS IN THE LATE 1890s were attracted to the physical remnants of their immediate communal past: the abandoned farmhouses, mills made redundant by the advent of steam power, cemeteries of early settlers. End-of-century reports give the overall impression of a landscape much tumbled down and tipped over, appealing rubble lying just off the beaten path. Visually compelling, stone ruins also opened the door to meditations on the passage of time and the double-edged nature of one hundred years of progress.

Ruins and remnants lie just off the beaten path of the staircase, as I begin to step down and out of the century that followed these writers'. The old, wooden stair itself was in ruinous shape before recently being replaced by galvanized steel. Stairs have always been a part of the landscape here, siege-ladders laid against the escarpment wall. Today, there are at least four flights at different locations in the city, all well-used—surprisingly well-used—by commuters, dog-walkers, exercisers, soccer teams in training, heart patients, non-drivers, students and wanderers.

A number of short stone towers stand on the scree slope of the escarpment, in a double line of tribute to the arts of masonry. They provided support for the tracks of an incline railway, a horizontal platform large enough to carry two horse-drawn buggies, as well as pedestrians, which until the 1930s provided an alternate way of travelling up and down.

An abandoned reservoir, also from the '30s, lies below, set against the slope. One of the concrete walls of this square, empty pool has a hole cut through it, which allows cars to enter and park beside a flat-roofed building. You can almost step onto the roof of the building, which is a small office, from the wall of the pool.

Liquid grey November returns in full force now, melds with the cool dampness that emanates from the exposed rock behind the steel stairs. Only the subtle bowl-shape of the rock indicates that water once fell over the escarpment edge at this spot. It's the old maps, again, that confirm the small hints in the lay of the land. As does the sound. As I near the bottom, the noise of traffic from six lanes of access road above and two lanes below is swallowed by the noise coming from the grates at the tops of a double line of what look like concrete silos. The crescendo of plunging water fills the air, the amplified sound of a captured stream as the stream falls the height of the escarpment through pipes buried in the ground.

A sense of age, abandonment and isolation pervades. This spot has had its day, several days, but those days are over. In the course of civic life some places keep within the orbit of attention while others fade, drift or fall away. This is Mercer's Glen, in the middle of the city. Hamilton. Oh, what do I care about your habits of habitation? I care for landscape, earth's shape. Yet I am attracted to these places of broken beauty, these abandoned parts of the broken body.

The stairway touches bottom, and the path continues beside a stone outbuilding, a stone wall, along the edge of the incline railway's former right-of-way. The right-of-way is the width of a city lot, narrow, and filled with a fallen crop of dead and drying weeds. Until I learn, later, that the site serves as the prime location for introducing native plants back into the area, and that the dead weeds represented a wild homecoming party winding down for the season, I don't know whether to laugh or cry when I read the small sign attached to a metal post at the end of this overgrown clearing. The irony seems savage. Or maybe someone *is* taking the long view, the glacially long view. The sign reads:

AREA

OF

NATURAL REGENERATION

# Submission to an Unannounced Competition for Proposals Toward a Vast and Total Redevelopment of Niagara Falls

*A seven year project*

### YEAR ONE

On the first day of the first year of this project, all vehicular and air traffic in and around the Falls is diverted or banned. Two assemblies gather at the edge of the Gorge, one on either side of the River. Each group divides into two. One of the resultant four groups proceeds south, upriver, another north, downriver, while the remaining two direct themselves west and east.

Each group walks until it is completely out of earshot of the "outrageous Noise, more terrible than that of Thunder." Since sound travels varying distances depending on atmospheric conditions and temperature, this initial ceremony will be performed four times, once at each solstice and equinox.

The four points farthest from the Falls at which silence is attained become the four points on the outside circumference of a circle. All redevelopment takes place within this circle. As sound travels farther downriver, and downwind, than up, its centre is anticipated to lie in the vicinity of the Whirlpool rather than at the Falls itself.

Father Hennepin wrote concerning the waters of this Prodigous Cascade, "when the Wind blows from off the South, their dismal roaring may be heard above fifteen Leagues off." A league being approximately five kilometres, the roaring then carried a distance of forty-five kilometres, which, forgive me, Father, seems an exaggeration, even for you. It should be noted from the outset, however, that exaggeration is considered an entirely appropriate response; indeed, it serves as this proposal's jumping-off point.

### YEAR TWO & THREE

All properties within the circle are purchased or expropriated.

### YEAR FOUR

All physical structures within the circle are dismantled and removed: gift shops, arcades, wax museums, casinos, restaurants, hotels, homes, etc. This list excludes only Thomas Barnett's Niagara Falls Museum. The museum is to be grandfathered, as we find Barnett's hodgepodge collection of artifacts and oddities, the hollowed redwood tree trunk, and the display under glass of hundreds of small stuffed birds that have perched upon their dead branches for several generations, compelling.

All else goes.

### YEAR FIVE

Infrastructure is dug up and removed. Watermains, sewers, roadways. Channels, reservoirs are filled in; electrical generating stations dismantled and removed. The increase in velocity as the Falls returns to full force will result in a greater volume of sound, which will require that the circle be enlarged.

The area within the circle is intended to be one of complete silence. Any aural infringement of its perimeter is dealt with in this fifth year of the proposal, by the rerouting of outside highway, road or rail.

### YEAR SIX

Using the earliest descriptions, diary sketches and maps obtainable, the area within the circle is re-landscaped to conform to its original contours. The pile of tumbled-down rock that lay at the base of the Falls, as evidence of the Falls' continued progress toward Lake Erie, is returned to its place.

Because the Falls is again at full force, its upriver advancement will be as rapid as it was before the advent of electrical generation. The circle's centre, as a result, will also move incrementally upriver over the years. It is proposed that the circle simply be enlarged to accomodate this shift.

YEAR SEVEN

The site is opened to the public. From parking lots provided outside the circumference, the public may breach the perimeeter of silence to enter the thunderous circle and approach the Falls on foot, or by means of any other non-motorized conveyance. The young, elderly, infirm, unable, unwilling or newlywed are offered baby carriage, stroller, horse and carriage, bicycle or wheelchair, free of charge.

A railing, one that combines function with aesthetics in its design, greets the crowd as they approach the edge of the Gorge.

POSTSCRIPT

After dutifully listening to this proposal—with its long walk from the perimeter of the circle to the cliff edge—prior to a family excursion to Niagara Falls one morning, the proposal author's twelve-year-old child asked,
"You're not going to make *us* do that, are you Dad?"

# Brother Nick and the Centre of the Earth

He was in the driver's seat, negotiating curve and slope at one hundred kilometres an hour as the highway slipped under the railway bridges, past Mercer's Glen and into the sudden embrace of Cootes Paradise, entering the city. You have to watch the road here. People have lost their lives to these curves and slopes. Isn't that just like home, making you feel safe and secure and all the while heightening the danger?

Cootes Paradise lay calm and flat, in its giant-reflecting-pool mood. As we crossed the bridge over the canal I indicated Princess Point, a promontory into the marsh, bordered by willows which hung over the water. The willows' light green is one of the first signs of spring, making the Point a beacon of seasonal change. In winter, Princess Point is the launch-site for skaters on the few days that the marsh actually freezes over. Archaeological digs there have unearthed enough unusual shards and artifacts to give name to a "Princess Point Culture." Nick knew all this as well as I did—even better, since his interest, inclination and profession was history. I had lately begun to suspect that some parts of the point were not natural, but landfill. But that wasn't what I wanted to show him.

At the very tip of the point, on a portion of shoreline free of willows, a small dock, only two or three metres long, supported by two metal posts, protruded into the water. In wet years, people fished from it; in dry, the posts stood in hardened mud.

"The centre of the earth," I said to my brother, pointing to the dock—which has since, incidentally, gone missing.

Perhaps I was trying to engage him in an imaginative flight that could bring together all the thoughts and feelings that I knew we both shared about this place, to land us somewhere near a truth about it. Instead, I tripped off the innocent, instinctual, brother-to-brother challenge of a verbal arm-wrestle.

"What do you mean?" he said.

The landscape rarely behaves as you expect it to. By this time, the area of the Iroquois Bar around the High Level Bridge had already proven itself to me as the centre of the surrounding landscape. From the perspective of the bridge itself, however, the landscape seemed to focus around the dock, as though from the centre of the landscape the focus became finer, even more particularized—the centre within the centre. Or perhaps, like the poles, one of them was true north, and stayed put, while the other, magnetic north, drifted across the landscape, slightly changing the reading on the compass.

The dock was the only object built by human hand on that side of the marsh. On the opposite side stood the shed from which Thomas B. McQuesten's canoe had emerged for the annual tool about Paradise. The shed's location had changed, though. It had been moved off the Bruntons' property and across the water when the highway came through. It had also been transformed from wooden boathouse to steel-sided box, as though the steel industry up the bay had tossed a line over the Bar to the marsh. A muted yet garish pale green, belligerently ignorant of where it stood. The dock reached a hand from earth to water, extending earth *over* water, connecting the two, suggesting the possibility of interplay, a humble commerce of memory and time, ourselves included. Something about what it might mean to live in this place.

"Yeah, but *the centre of the earth?*"

I was talking to a man who had once proposed that a jet of water shooting up from the middle of the bay would be a marvelous way to turn the bay into an enormous, civic fountain, a natural version of the wrought iron fountain that stood downtown. Surely he understood that such formal and less formal intrusions into the landscape—his fountain, my dock—were ways of ordering our attachment to the physical environment, of providing a centre for our relation to it. He'd done research on Thomas B. McQuesten, after all, written the paper that first connected the man's work rehabilitating the Iroquois Bar to the wider, City Beautiful movement. Thomas B, our mutual hero, who more than anyone had turned the civic eye toward its natural surroundings.

"Well, it's a nice metaphor," he said, in response to my tongue-tied silence.

I understood my statement to have been dismissed as poetry, which is to say neither true nor false; a pleasant, if exaggerated way of looking at things. Nick had every right to put me in my place, if that's what he was doing. I felt chastened. I had delivered a bald statement, thinking its meaning would be self-evident to the sympathetic hearer, but could not give substance to the feeling behind the statement.

Nick swung us up the exit ramp and into the city: all these rectilinear divisions, all this parcelling-up into precise allotments, streets and buildings, pavement and brick.

*I don't want metaphor*, I thought but did not say. *I want the thing itself.*

# Selective Memory: The Doll's Leg

GARBAGE-PICKERS DID what their name suggests. Wandering the streets in the 1930s, they picked through the cans at the side of the road and in the alleys, looking for things edible or saleable. The controversy at City Hall and in the newspapers about allowing or disallowing the activity was tempered by the fact that these were hard times and people needed whatever they could find.

My mother called me a garbage-picker. I liked to rove the alleys behind our house and along the route I took home from school, and though I don't recall actually picking through the soggy bags in someone's trash can, I do recall lifting lids and finding things. Once I came upon a tiny pocket knife, a real treasure, but promptly dropped it into a puddle, and then tried to bail out the puddle with a tin can, as cars with amused adults behind their windows drove past where I squatted in the mud. At five years, I was as yet unaware of my ethnic heritage; the can could not accomplish what a windmill might have. The knife was forever lost to the muddy pool, or to the next finder.

Another day, I flew home from school through the back

alley at an estimated altitude of four hundred feet, or shoulder height, holding firmly between thumb and forefinger the plastic, pencil-sharpening airplane I'd just found, and piloting a wide course around the puddled lakes below.

English was my mother's second language, and I think she must have picked up the term garbage-picker without its wet sack of history, without knowing what, other than the literal, it might imply. Such as poverty. Destitution. A lack of goods and comestibles. Though our family was immigrant and not wealthy, the term described a socio-economic condition we were unfamiliar with. I understood the compound word coming from her lips simply as she meant it, a descriptive term for what I was inclined to do, and though she never actually forbade my pursuit, it never made her list of preferred activities.

I'm still at it, Mom.

You pick and choose objects from the store shelf, the yard-sale table or the garbage because they speak to you, regardless of what they say or don't say to others. Want is implied: the want of lack, of desire. The objects are useable, they serve a real need; or they are superfluous, decorative. Or they perform some dance for the imagination. Mary and I furnished our first apartment on Sunday evenings, in pre-garbage-day forays along the streets of wealthier neighbourhoods. We lived among the debris of interiors greater than our own. Twenty-five years later we still have the leaded-glass window, framed and hanging where the light can pass through, that we claimed one such evening. It was an object of our choosing. I've wondered if it can work the other way, and an object choose us. We invest them with meaning; can they invest their possible meanings with us?

## Selective Memory: The Doll's Leg

AT LEAST TWICE, while traipsing around on Burlington Heights, I'd walked past the plastic doll where it lay in the tall grass just past the High Level Bridge. I was still somewhat ambivalent about picking up lost or tossed articles, and intent on being selective about which ones I stooped for. Choosing my meanings, so to speak. A plastic naked baby didn't suit the symbolic decor that was beginning to collect on the bookshelf. "The sacramental power of objects given or received in the right spirit?" Spare me.

The third time I saw the doll, I was with a friend. As we walked along, Glenn told me about a video recording that friends of his had made in a large, abandoned warehouse. They'd found a metre-high statue of Jesus in the middle of the glass-strewn, concrete floor. They'd stood him up and smashed him to bits with bricks and boards, while documenting the destruction on tape. Watching the playback, Glenn had gotten mad at them. He said no one should ever take a found object and simply destroy it.

The forcefulness of his opinion surprised me more than the smashing. I frankly didn't see anything terribly reprehensible in the act. His friends were in a setting that was already, by definition, garbage—the warehouse was slated for demolition. Who hasn't, with great satisfaction, shattered their share of glass or ceramics? Perhaps it's the Protestant in me that's reluctant to give physical objects any more than a physical, or monetary, worth. As a group, we Protestants started off by breaking and destroying a few things, I seem to recall. Glenn is a thoughtful person, though, and I couldn't just dismiss what he was saying.

We'd already walked past the spot where the doll had been lying, and I'd noticed it was missing. A city works crew had been out earlier in the day, and the grass along the ramp was now cut, so it seemed likely the workers had picked up roadside debris during the course of their labours, baby included.

At the end of the Heights we watched the carp roil in the still water below the bridge, then began to walk back, stopping at the same break in the black willows where my equinoctial vigil had taken place. Overlooking Cootes Paradise, Glenn related a second story, one he said he hadn't yet told to anyone.

His brother, Colin, was a painter, teacher, conservationist and avowed anti-car activist. To Colin, the car was the source of more social and environmental ills than it could ever be worth. He rode his bike year-round, till the icicles formed on the hood of his jacket, although he did allow himself to put his bike into the trunk of my car once and accept a ride in a downpour. He wasn't an ideologue. And he couldn't bicycle his two children five hundred kilometres home to their mother on New Year's Day last winter, in conditions of ice and snow. The crash occurred on that trip. A car coming from the opposite direction slid on black ice, crossed the median, and struck the driver's side of his car. His two children were badly injured, and Colin was killed.

The following summer Glenn decided to make the two-hundred-kilometre journey from where he was living in Peterborough, home to his parents in Hamilton. He rode Colin's well-travelled bike, plotting the route so that he would pedal past the scene of the accident. Neither Glenn nor anyone in the family had visited the crash site, and a kind of gaping hole existed in their lives where Colin had been wrenched away. The police had given the family everything they'd picked up after the accident, but the ground had been covered in snow and it would have been easy to miss something. Glenn wanted to see if he could find the spot where the violence to Colin and their family—to their whole, extended family—had taken place; if perhaps any of Colin's belongings still lay at the side of the road.

He knew the road and general location of the crash, nothing more. He asked at a gas station if anyone remembered the accident on New Year's Day. What accident? No, they didn't. Try the fire station. He asked at the fire station. Same response. He tried several other gas stations and businesses before it became clear to him that for anyone who worked along Airport Road in Toronto, one accident was impossible to distinguish from the next, there were so many. He decided simply to bike down the road and keep his eyes open, reconciled to whatever he might or might not find.

Not far along, a flash of white blinked at him from the ditch. He guided his bike down the embankment, reached out his arm, and, before even picking it up, recognized the flash as belonging to Colin. A lapel button, which served as the admission ticket to a day-long festival called "The Whole Lot," the last event Colin had participated in as a painter and performer, three months before the accident. Glenn had missed Colin's performance because he himself had been performing at the same event, at the same time, in a different venue.

Glenn looked around. He found a game piece nearby: a plastic medieval tournament horse from Colin's son's Christmas present. Colin's daughter's Christmas novel, *The Girl from Away*. A package of child-support cheques, signed, postdated for the year ahead. Colin's daybook. Two audio tapes,

*Fumbling Towards Ecstasy* and another whose case opened to a poem in which a person wants to have wings like an angel keeps feeling their shoulder blades to see if wings have started growing.

Unlike some of us, Glenn doesn't necessarily feel compelled to squeeze every last drop of universal meaning from events in his life, but he had been looking to put together some of the fragments of the lives that had been shattered by the accident that took his brother, and was given a selection of debris that had been jettisoned from Colin's car on impact, personal articles still lying on the ground months later. I understood now why he'd been so upset with his friends' smashing of Jesus. That Jesus was symbolic of all anonymous objects. Glenn had showed a lot of trust in biking down that road.

THE NEXT DAY I HIKED back to the ramp to see if the naked plastic doll was anywhere to be found. Perhaps the city works crew had tossed the baby not into the bin but over the guardrail.

Poking through the grass and weeds. Nothing. Then I spotted a short, chubby, half-bent leg, seven centimetres long. A single, baby doll body part. I stared at it, and before my eyes the rest of the body began to materialize. It was the doll that had been lying in the grass before, its face looking up with familiar cheerfulness, as though waiting for a diaper to be changed. My eyes were filling in the blank left by the missing body. When they returned to the leg actually lying on the ground, it came back to me: the doll I passed twice before had been missing a limb. This was that missing limb. The leg likely had come detached from the body on impact with the ground, when the doll first came flying out of a passing car.

I remembered Mary asking what it meant, this doll on the ground, and wondering whose doll it was, what the story had been from inside the car. I bent to pick up the limb, realizing that I'd been filling in the blank each time I'd passed the doll's body, too, making a visual jump that made the one-legged, naked baby doll lying on the side of the road whole in my mind. But the body never had been whole, it was broken the first time I laid eyes on it.

The body was broken to begin with.

# A Gruesome Ground

THE GREAT GREY EGG of the cholera stone sits on top of its tumulus, its terp, like one of those anomalous rocks that the glaciers leave behind in farmers' fields, which have to be ploughed around for generations because they're simply too large to move. An erratic.

Or like one of the stones that native Canadians placed under the tongue, to keep their mouths moist during their long-distance running-walks on the paths that networked the countryside and the continent. A stone for a giant, long-distance walker.

Lately the memorial has been bathed in the evenings in the orange glow from a highway lamp standard. The highway is fifteen or twenty metres below the level of the cholera stone, while the tower of light extends an equal distance above it. The pole is one in a newly-planted line of poles placed giant steps apart on the median between the east and westbound lanes of traffic. The poles replace the much shorter street lights that used to line the road on either side. Before this pole was erected, it was dark around this stone at night, and I would have hesitated to come here.

237

*Let light perpetual shine on them.*

To anyone of a literalist frame of mind, the orange glow recalls the liturgical line in the mass for the dead. Here, the dead are just below one's feet. Is "light perpetual" what the highway designers had in mind when locations for the new lamp standards were decided upon in the offices of the provincial Ministry of Highways? This particular post is itself about to become a memory. A jogger of Burlington Heights who regularly uses the cholera terp for a mid-run pause-and-view was appalled at how the huge post and its blossom of lights intruded on the view of Cootes Paradise and Dundas Valley. He was sufficiently upset to pound loudly on the right doors, inviting Ministry officials and politicians and the newspaper to come and see for themselves. Everyone agreed. The post is in the wrong place. The Minister has promised it shall be moved.

*Guard This Resting Place*, says the plaque on the cholera stone.

*Cholera Stone*

*A Gruesome Ground*

The new lamp standards along the median were themselves erected out of a kind of respect for the dead—for the more recently departed, rather than the ones below the stone. They are intended to help keep the living alert. More than one person has come flying along the sloping curves of the highway below, entering the city late at night, and lost control of their car just at that moment when their vehicle leaving the road would find the narrow slot between the east and westbound bridges over the Desjardins canal, and dive into the water. Most have drowned. After the last such crash, a major effort was made to prevent this from happening again. The highway was widened, concrete barriers were put up, and the new lighting standards erected. All of it a huge, earth-moving, re-landscaping, permanent, unplaqued memorial.

Standing down by the canal's edge, gazing up at the sky through the slot of daylight between the two highway bridges, you wonder how they did it. It seems an almost impossible feat to have found that slot.

Burlington Heights collects death. The bridge support on the far side of the canal carries a sign:

DANGER
NO SWIMMING
STRONG CURRENTS HAVE CAUSED
THE DROWNING OF 4 PERSONS
IN THIS CANAL SINCE 1971

Shortly after friends of ours moved to the area, they took a canoe onto Cootes Paradise and were paddling about, when they came near the canal and saw a number of policemen, and a police diver who, they were told, was searching the water for two missing people. Brothers, who'd been fishing together when one fell in, and the other had jumped in to save him.

"You might want to keep paddling," the police said. Nice introduction to the city, thought these friends.

How did George and Al Mercer and all the other children survive, swinging out over the water from willow trees and falling into the canal? Often as not, they didn't. Anyone who used to swim there mentions the strong current in the canal. The wail of an ambulance regularly filled the air when she was growing up, Margaret Brunton said, and it frequently meant that another child had drowned. Like her playmate, who disappeared into the suddenly deeper water of the old canal channel just off the point by the Bruntons' home. Or the three-year-old who ran and tripped off the dock of one of the boathouses, into the canal. Chic Collura jumped into the Desjardins from the High Level Bridge and swam to shore, winded but kicking. More recently, two men jumped off the lower railway bridge into the canal late one drunken night, and only one of them made it to shore.

The railway was the scene of a major accident in 1857, when the engine of the train from Toronto snapped an axle as the train approached an earlier version of the bridge over the canal. The engine broke through the bridge, pulling the passenger cars with it into the water. Sixty-nine people died. The *Illustrated News* published a series of lithographs of the accident and its aftermath, for at the time this was the deadliest train crash in the world.

Death by water, death by land. During the construction of the railway, a number of workers died when a portion of the embankment they were digging collapsed on them.

Forty years earlier, seven men were hanged on the Heights.

As transplanted Americans living on Upper Canadian soil, their ambivalence over who was foe and who friend during the War of 1812 inspired activities helpful to the official enemy, which led to charges of treason. Eighteen were charged, eight convicted. Seven were publicly hanged on the Heights in 1813, the eighth died when the gallows beam fell on him prior to execution.

And then there is the grey egg of the cholera stone itself. Beneath it lie soldiers from the War of 1812, who were joined twenty years later, and then twenty years again after that, by the victims of the two cholera epidemics that hit the city. The epidemics struck much of the continent, and port towns like Hamilton were especially susceptible because the disease often arrived by boat. Most of the victims were recently-landed immigrants who had contracted the waterborne disease during the crossing. To help forestall its epidemic spread to the general population, the new arrivals were temporarily housed in the warehouses near the docks, or taken to the old British military barracks on Burlington Heights, where they could be housed and, if necessary, hospitalized. And where they soon came to be buried in lime-lined mass graves, because the disease did, in fact, break out despite precautions. Horse-drawn carts transported them, the still-living on their pallets, the dead lying in boxes stacked on the beds of the wagons.

An old soldier stationed at the entrance to the quarantined site sat in his chair, leaning against the ramshackle barrack that was his home. When asked by a reporter if he did not fear catching the disease, he declared that he "cared neither for the devil nor the cholera." Beside him stood an open barrel, inside of which were curled his two pet rattlesnakes.

The deceased immigrants were buried on a point overlooking Cootes Paradise—their only view of the paradise they had crossed an ocean to find. Their small community lies only a little down the road from the cemetery, city of the dead, where more than eighty thousand lie, settlers and other immigrants, their descendants.

THE CHOLERA STONE and its plaque were dedicated early in the twentieth century, so they were not yet in place when a reporter came to the Heights in 1897, doing research for the series of stories the newspaper was running in an end-of-century overview of the area—stories that give the impression of stone ruins lying everywhere about, the whole place in a kind of evocative shambles.

No ponderable remnants graced the Heights, though. The writer begins,

> Not anywhere in or near the city of Hamilton is it at all likely that a more historically gruesome ground can be found than that around Burlington Heights and the Desjardins Canal ... The other day a farmer, plowing in a field on the side of the heights over the canal, unearthed a skeleeton ...
>
> If there is any place about the city where spirits should come from their graves at midnight and flit about in the darkness it is the heights.

A sketch artist accompanied the reporter, as did the artist's young daughter. The reporter led them to the cholera cemetery.

> ... No drearier spot could be found for a burying ground. Perhaps a dozen fir trees are there; stunted and forlorn looking, their branches sighing in the wind as in keeping with the eternal fitness of things. To the west from the cemetery the marsh lies in the hollow and the snakelike canal shows itself through the rush bed maze. Mists rise from the dead waters in early morning and night and malaria and fever seem to breed there. Not a head stone shows in the cemetery; even the fences are down.

The place had the feeling of exposed remoteness, open isolation, that it is possible to experience still today, even as traffic whizzes by.

> "What are these little hills, papa?" asked the Spectator artist's little girl as she jumped from one to another.
> "They are graves," she was told, and at once she stopped her jumping and was serious.
> "And what are those holes?" she asked again, pointing to somewhat larger hollows.
> "They are graves, too," was the reply.
> "That big hole, too?" she queried again, in wonderment, pointing to a hollow fully fifteen feet square.
> "Yes."
> "Oh, papa, nobody ever was as big as that," she replied, incredulous.

A few years ago I stopped on the lazy, hairpin turn of Old Guelph Road to see what all the commotion was about on Chedoke highway below. A couple of badly damaged cars and a large transport trailer were beside the exit ramp for York Boulevard. What looked at first like the smashed front end of the transport truck turned out to be the flattened remains of another vehicle. Piecing the shards of a story together from various drivers, the police later concluded that an elderly couple had missed the exit, panicked, stopped, and then began to back up. The transport truck swerved to avoid the backing-up car and hit someone else instead. The couple was not involved in the crash. They drove away, doomed to re-live the episode from that day on—or are living in sweet forgetfulness.

The reporter concludes,

> This, in brief, is the history of the heights, not perhaps complete in detail, but fairly correct in general outline.

From the end of the promontory where the stone sits bathed in the orange glow of the new light standard of the highway, white lights can be seen of traffic coming down the side of the escarpment several kilometres away. The stream of lights seems almost processional. Judging by the highway and its eternal illumination, the two things we most can't stand are the two most closely associated with death: darkness and silence. The cars will be here in a moment, rubbing up against the side of the giant who took the stone out of his mouth and placed it at this spot where memory resides, where he ended his long walk and lay his broken body down.

Nobody was ever as big as that.

Driving, we are metaphors for our own transience, hurtling through the night air in the waiting room of our destination, the dream-chamber of a car, sailing over land and through time, occasionally launching ourselves into air and water, or causing others to be launched.

In almost the same moment that they arrive, the cars are gone.

# Falling into Place

IN A RECURRING DREAM from childhood, I am falling. The dream is a strange, exciting and gentle one. I am standing on the top of a bare hill, surrounded by other round, bare hills. I look down, and when I do, I lose my balance and begin to fall. But the fall is horizontal. It's very much like flying, though without any flapping of arms or wings on my part. Dreams of flying, in youth, are supposed to be about sexual awakening. As are bare, round hills, I'll bet. I was twelve or thirteen years old at the time, so an awakening would make sense. Okay. Let the recurring dream be about sexuality. Let it be about pleasure and sensuality, about big physical desires, bodily contact, union and release, as manifested in the pure, floating weightlessness of a single sleeping individual, who is young. And let the earth and air be the precincts of that dream.

I never landed, that I recall. While fall-flying I knew that the end would mean contact with the ground, and wondered if the landing would be soft or if I would die. Soft, I thought. Did I have some notion of the earth's fundamental kindness? I was already defying gravity. Which other basic laws of nature did I expect would be bent for the sake of my dreams?

The landscape of round, bare hills that existed in the dream was drawn from an actual place, though I didn't discover this fact until thirty years later. My family often spent two summer weeks living out of a house trailer beside a lake in the Okanagan Valley. The Okanagan lies between ranges of the Rocky Mountains, a landscape of long, narrow lakes stretched end to end, nudged on both sides by tan-coloured hills. Travelling there again with my wife and family I recognized those arid hills as that long-ago dreamscape. I realized, too, that the dreamscape of my youthful sleeping was a modified version of the actual, physical landscape. In the dreams there were no lakes, and the hills of the Okanagan were greened, bare but grassy.

Memories are surprisingly physical, as I found out in returning to the Okanagan. They can knock the wind out of you and bend you double, not necessarily from pain or pleasure, but from nothing more than the simple re-concurrence of place and person. And dreams take what they need or please from memory and desire, from the body of earth and the human body, to create a landscape that fits their own purposes. Or perhaps a landscape imposes itself on the sleeping individual, without respect for geographical or personal time periods.

More recently, my present landscape of sandbar, escarpment, marsh and bay has made an appearance in my sleep, only now I am swimming, not flying. I stroke through the body of water on one side of the sand-and-gravel bar, water much too shallow to swim in reality, then through the canal cut and into the body of water on the other. Both the Iroquois Bar and the surrounding, low hills are as bare and lightly tanned as the hills of the Okanagan Valley. Very much like human flesh, in fact, seen up close. Their surface is pebbled, like naked skin exposed to the outside air, or responding to touch: goosebumps.

The dream has altered the actual landscape this time, too. Or it's given me a landscape much older than the present one, and superimposed the two. The goosebumps are the sand and gravel, pebble and cobble that become visible wherever the surface of the Bar has been exposed by scraping or digging, but to expose them the dream has had to denude the sandbar of both its foliage and the accumulated soil of twelve thousand years. The landscape hasn't been so bare since the glaciers left town.

We've returned to sex and the grown-up twelve-year-old, still dreaming. The landscape as lover—but not really. The landscape as loved, and loving; as a physicality the grown-up doesn't want to be separated from. What the twelve-year-old has returned to is the body, which is where he wanted to be in the first place.

MY PERSONAL MEMORY of this place begins when I landed here a couple of decades ago, a single generation. If the bits of historical or geographical knowledge I have picked up and accumulated since, together with my experiences of the place, alone or with others, constitute my memory of it, then perhaps memory is built up in the same way the sand-and-gravel bar was, one stone at a time: one small stone for each day, for each story, a stone for each time the foot makes contact with the ground. I may have managed by now to construct a layer or two this way, like the layers of the Bar, but the top of my bar is still only slightly above water level. Which is as it should be, because this memorizing is no more a *fait accompli* than the Iroquois Bar was, and is. Creation goes on. The waters meet and play this beach as if they still had all the time in the world.

And the stones: some are from hereabouts, some aren't. They come from almost anywhere. Anywhere handy to the dream glacier that collects and deposits them. The specifics of my own memory include this place itself and other places: ones I am connected to by experience, such as the Okanagan, and ones I am connected to through past generations, race, such as the landscape of Friesland. The Bar of my own memory is made, is created, out of this relation between the earth and myself, between its body and my own, in dream and desire.

Understand that this is a landscape I love, the one I have adopted, or that has adopted me, that reveals itself to me over time in a kind of slow, affectionate undressing. There is no way to explain this love of place other than to say that I want to be here. I want to move through the various folds and creases, to travel the falls and rises, every square inch, and to stand wherever I am; wherever, by this gracious allowance, I am granted leave to stop and dwell upon and within what surrounds me, to see and touch what this physical familiarity reveals and gives. And familiarity is a powerful aphrodisiac. This is as true for a person who has lived in a certain physical landscape long enough to feel its contours call response from their own physical being as it is for a person who anticipates returning to the one from whom love has been received, from whom love will be received again.

There are other slow undressings. The infant's. The plastic baby doll in play with a small child, or the flesh and blood baby placed upon the change table by the mother or father, who removes the articles of clothing on a purely utilitarian and necessary pretext, but also for pleasure, in order to see and to touch again that loved, bare body.

Or the undressing comes later, administered by the now mature child who returns this attention when the age-tables are turned and the cared-for becomes caregiver. When the child sponge-bathes the body of a mother or father no longer able to do so for herself, himself. When ancestor becomes eternal child. When the life under your hand is older, more layered, and has carried its wounds longer than your own. The body, broken to begin with, is ageless.

It is also naked to begin with. Slowly clothed in time and place, it flies naked at last again. It is a gift to look over the whole body of earth and know where, on falling, you wish your own body to land, and lie.

# A Slow Undressing

GUARD THIS RESTING PLACE of unknown soldiers, sailors and immigrants; of stones arranged by glaciers' waters: the sand and gravel, pebble and cobble. Give voice to this beleaguered Bar. *Tell them. Say.*

Is the landscape speaking? Oh please, I'm not going to start hearing the landscape now, am I?

I am back sitting in the car, looking out on Mercer's Glen from the shelter of the tunnel under Chedoke highway. I've managed to park on the very narrow shoulder of the road inside the tunnel. Flat, grey concrete is my wall and ceiling. It's raining. A curtain of water drapes entry and egress, as if I'm in the middle of a double-sided waterfall. A stream runs audibly in the gutter outside the car window. This was the only place for someone who normally smokes outdoors to keep dry while indulging. Bad habits occasionally reveal a redemptive aspect. In this case, the urge sent its habitee, me, to a location he otherwise might not have visited, to see what he otherwise would not have seen.

A funeral procession drove past as I stood between liquid curtains, against the tunnel wall. Twenty cars, entering and exiting, passing my involuntary honour guard and slowly ascending the curving pavement to the top of the Heights. It seemed disrespectful to be smoking, so I put the cigarette out. I'd never seen a funeral pass this way before; it's off their beaten path, and more than one of the mourners and friends asked me with their car-window glances the same question I was asking them:

What are *you* doing here?

*I am standing out of the rain,* is what I am doing. *I am in active suppression of strong emotion through the agency of tobacco,* is what. *I am pausing for shelter from the downpour of events that have befallen this place.*

ANOTHER ASSAULT is being prepared against the Iroquois Bar. In the newspaper this morning were the plans and latest political pushing and posturing for a new highway that would connect the industry farther up the bay with Chedoke highway along Cootes Paradise. The Perimeter Road. It would run on the railway lands below Dundurn Castle, and then enter a tunnel under the Iroquois Bar and the cemetery, on its way to union with the present highway. In an alternative plan, it barrels through the Desjardins canal cut. The idea, in whatever form, has been around for a number of years: the Boar storming out of the Welsh King Arthur story, that would ravage this landscape. Normally the multi-laned beast sleeps under the heavy blanket of fiscal restraint, but occasionally, unexpectedly, it raises its tusked head from under the covers and snorts, as it did again today.

*Why can't the Bar just be left alone?*

One day, I detected a pattern in the abuse of the Iroquois Bar. An operation of one kind or another had been performed upon it in each generation since settlement began, when Richard and Henrietta Beasley first stuck shovel in ground, chopped tree and began disassembling a landscape of oak savannah to accommodate their long-term stay. Theirs was a comparatively benign re-landscaping, all told, to which I do not object, much. It undid only the achievement of generations of trees.

Twenty-some years later the British Army set up camp, dug and threw up earthworks at two locations, cut native as well as orchard trees for building and firewood, built barracks and hospitals, and generally ran amok over the entire length of the Burlington Heights half of the Bar. Allan MacNab's arrival twenty years after the war also brought major changes to the landscape. But the first truly mammoth earth-moving project waited until twenty years after MacNab began to build Dundurn, when the railway came with grade-levelling, landfill and canal cut. Forty years later, just before the century ended, a second railway was built along the Cootes Paradise side. Two decades into the new century, the first generation of roadways and bridges designed for the automobile was constructed; a second generation of six-lane, limited access highway, came thirty years after that.

We're pushing thirty-five, forty years after the highway's construction. Unless the cycle has been broken, I thought, we're due.

A new, commuter railway line had just been laid, adding a sixth bridge to the five that already spanned the canal cut. Also, the carp dam had been finished. Even more recently, a wide, paved walking path had been built along the bay shoreline, through the Desjardins canal cut, to Princess Point. All three of these involved earth-moving alterations, though the third was unusual, in being the most positive intrusion on the landscape since McQuesten's beautification projects, and one that involved no landfill. The moment the path opened, hordes of city folk returned to a waterfront they hadn't been able to come near for at least two generations.

Would these changes suffice?

When I mentioned the pattern to someone who'd been a member of the committee that campaigned for the restoration of the High Level Bridge, against official plans calling for its replacement, he reminded me of the Perimeter Road. Ah, of course. How could I have forgotten? Now, a scant few weeks later, the article appears in the paper.

SOME OF US RELY on the visible world more than others. Our physical surroundings mean something to us. It makes a difference that houses and buildings are where they are and look as they do, that fences and trees have the particular arrangement we wind our ways through every day, that the bridge carries us across the canal, and the low hills roll beside the road as we leave the city, that there is a tall wall of rock in our backyard with a staircase laid against it, a finger of land pointing into the bay, or a tongue of water extending into the beach. All this is the larger furniture of our lives; the public, shared version of the objects we gather to live amongst in our homes. For no other reason than that they exist and are familiar, these details of the outside world seem to us to have as much right to their place in the landscape as we do ourselves. They provide the physical context in which we live our lives. When one of them is taken away or changed, we are affected, diminished.

Now, if the fence is decayed or the tree dead, if the building is truly beyond salvation or the road requires upgrading, we may not mind what happens next, may even applaud. But it depends. It depends on whether the replacement or change recognizes, has some feeling and thought for the place itself and for the community it belongs to, because community here includes these objects: it includes the objects of our own making as well as those of the natural world.

All of these physical things are symbols of our life together, and as such have a meaning that we share, even if our interpretation of that meaning differs. When the buildings come down and changes are made that don't show care for place, that dare us to continue caring, or that make a mockery of our attachment, it's as though we are being told—we who rely on the visible world—that we are living a lie.

TOWARD THE END of the time of my fly-falling dreams, I read the novel *Little Big Man*, by Thomas Berger. The story took place on the Great Plains, and told about the slow assault on native life and culture by waves of railway, American troops and the growing army of immigrant whites from the east. Based on his observation of these new arrivals to the landscape, the main native character, a chief named Old Lodge Skins, tells Little Big Man, a white who has been adopted by the tribe, that he believes whites have a reason for what they do, but they are a strange people who do not seem to know where the centre of the world is.

Later, with a few more year's experience of whites and their ways under his belt, Lodge Skins expands on the observation. He tells Little Big Man that Human Beings (the translation of his tribe's name, Cheyenne) believe everything is alive: men and animals, water and earth and stones, and also those who have died. Whites, on the other hand, believe everything is dead: everything, including their own people. And if things persist in trying to live, they will be rubbed out.

Why continue to beat the Iroquois Bar, generation after generation, if it is already dead? Are we not sure that it *is* dead? Perhaps that's what's behind the pattern: an honest-to-God fear that the earth actually lives. That it persists, is only sleeping. And each generation must reassert itself, make certain, to its own satisfaction, that victim remains victim, that sleeper never wakes.

The first bridge to span the canal cut was a wooden suspension bridge. A September storm came in 1857, three years after the bridge was built. The wind funnelling through the cut was strong enough to lift the bridge from underneath and cause it to wave, more and more wildly, until it was literally flung apart, sending planking into the canal below—as though the arm of the Bar was shaking itself free.

The sleeper stirring.

Tuck two fingers under a railway tie in the tracks below Dundurn Castle, pull up, watch the spikes pop out like buttons all the way to the end of the Iroquois Bar.

Step over the Bar. Repeat on marsh-side rails.

Sidestep to highway, roll up the carpet runners of three-lane pavement on one side of the median, three-lane pavement on the other side. Climb the Bar to the Boulevard, repeat the rolling.

Pluck all six bridges from their span over the canal cut. Place them in a box, in a closet. The children have finished playing, are tidying up. For the grandparents are coming.

There is some satisfaction to be found in these acts of the

restorative imagination, this redress. In this slow undressing. In seeing yourself the size at which it becomes possible.

Place the snout of a vacuum hose into the pond at Mercer's Glen; draw the mud, as through a straw, across Old Guelph Road into Cootes Paradise.

Ladle away the landfill of roadbed, rail bed.

Scoop the stuff taken from the Bar when the canal was cut into a big pile. Call friend, neighbour. Tell them, *Bring a lunch. Bring dinner.* Together, engage in the painstaking process known to archaeologists, diggers for dinosaurs, pickers of garbage. With giant hands, handle, sift these small stones. When the stones are sorted by size into piles, reassemble within the cut the layers of sand and gravel, pebble and cobble. Rise. Stand back. Watch water build behind the Bar.

As once you may have helped the beach's stream to breach a childhood vacation morning's dam of sand, stone and driftwood, now trace a finger through the channel which the glacial streams and currents crafted around the end of Iroquois Bar. Push through the two false digits of railway landfill.

Free the waters.

Jump in.

LITTLE BIG MAN was made into a movie. Toward the end of the movie, Old Lodge Skins decides that it is a good day to die. Being old and blind, he is helped by Little Big Man, the adopted white son who has blown in and out of his life like a fallen leaf. The chosen place is the crest of a hill. There, Old Lodge Skins raises his face and arms to the sky and slowly turns a complete circle as he thanks the Great Spirit for his long life, for having created him a Human Being, for having made him into a great warrior. In his praise he also gives thanks for the blindness which helped him to see more clearly, and for the path that the Spirit has chosen for the Human Beings to walk now, a path "which leads nowhere." He then lies down on the ground and closes his eyes to sleep.

The deep creases of his face, a landscape in itself, relax. Lodge Skins is a beautiful old man, and remarkably cheerful. He has experienced the destruction of a way of life and the near-extermination of a people, but he wears the world lightly. Native peoples and cultures have become the metaphor for what we as an immigrant European culture have lost in relation to the earth, and watching the movie I can't help but feel it is to salve the conscience of the white audience that this representative native person remains so spiritually whole and undiminished.

We wait for him to sleep. A storm has been gathering, and when its first raindrops fall, his face twitches involuntarily. Little tremors of flesh. Old Lodge Skins stirs, raises his head and asks aloud, "Am I still in the land of the living?" Little Big Man, who has been standing there the whole time, watching and waiting, answers him, "Yes you are, Grandfather." Lodge Skins utters a disappointed and miffed, "Eeeeh!" and lays his head down again. Soon, though, that smile of good cheer reanimates his face. He opens his blind eyes and as Little Big Man helps him to his feet Lodge Skins says, laughing, "Sometimes the magic works, and sometimes it doesn't."

The old native then leans upon his adopted son and the two walk down the hill in the pouring rain.

In the fable of the motion picture, the ancient native culture survives and goes on its indomitable, humourous, affectionate and non-judgmental way, leaning on a sobered, more self-aware, compassionate white.

In the novel, by contrast, Lodge Skins strips himself naked to stand on the hilltop, face the four directions and give praise to the Great Spirit. When he lies down he is allowed the dignity of accomplishing what he set out to do, that good day. He dies. The sober reality is that native culture as it existed on the Great Plains is dead, and Little Big Man is alone and bereft.

Years later Little Big Man is still alone, an ancient soul in a retirement home, the oddball who doesn't get along with others. And still bereft. He tells this story for the first time to an anthropologist, into a tape recorder. Soon after the telling, he dies.

SOMETIMES YOU CHOOSE your endings. Sometimes you find yourself staring blindly through falling drops, the curtains of water that drape the open ends of a tunnel, trying to keep your humour up, to keep dry while sending out little smoke offerings. Watching the body, waiting for the impossible moment when, under the impact of those drops, the flesh faintly quivers.

# Flight and Refuge

I HAVE ALWAYS WANTED to sense a Native presence here. Ghosts and spirits, some ineffable aura. I've always wanted to be able to tell that others lived here who, during their long tenure, did not move hills, fill in waterways, alter shorelines, or amputate arms of geography. Typical romantic yearnings from an urban and post-industrial vantage point, I suppose. Flight from the present into the refuge of the past.

There are places where it isn't hard to imagine such a presence, and to imagine that it existed for centuries. Specific spots have a stronger feel about them, though whether this has anything to do with the lives and deaths of our predecessors on the landscape, or is a result of a coincidence of geography and weather which may also have attracted those native ancestors, is anyone's guess. Where Bar meets escarpment, where Old Guelph Road touches the water level of the marsh: rock, water, trees and the elements of the air meeting in one place. A conversation goes on in these places, and if one is lucky and stands still long enough, they may even enter the conversation.

Or I'm making this up. Even in those special places, a little, nattering voice-in-the-head will argue that whatever is seen or heard amounts to no more than wish fulfillment. So be it. How could one hear the conversation if they didn't desire the ears for it, or enter, if they didn't desire the tongue? The enterprise is entirely voluntary. I hug only the occasional tree, but a tree alone has a terrific amount to say to anyone who would stand beneath and attend.

Any place truly loved and attended to will respond in kind. At the very least, it will show and tell itself in the ways that the people who live there speak about it, in how they think about it, what they draw and write. For me, the desire to sense a native presence in the landscape is, in part, a desire to feel indigenous to this place, and wondering what it would take to experience true belonging.

TOWARD THE END of the nineteenth century, people stood under the family-tree of settlement, gave it a good hug, and found that the tree did indeed have a lot to say. They gazed into the branches of the preceding, hundred years, and began to write. They wrote from a sense of ownership, of having lived in this one spot for so long—but only so long. A city had grown, from the ground, and these were the grandchildren of the first settlers retelling their grandparents' stories. They were also looking to fill in the blank in their knowledge of what this place was like *before* their grandparents' arrival.

Native burial mounds were still being uncovered during ploughing, and many people had assembled private collections of bones and arrowheads, tools and artifacts. Amateur anthropologists toured the countryside, giving illustrated lectures. In the broader culture of the time, ethnographers had begun to document and publish all they could discover about native peoples. Relationships were unravelled and explained, relationships between the various native groups and tribes who were spread over the entire continent, and who were as ethnically distinct from each other as were any number of European national groups, and who were *also* a mix of immigrants, refugees and adoptees, from other tribes, many of whom were no longer living anywhere near their original lands.

The Neutral nation lived at this western end of Lake Ontario when the first Europeans, Jesuit missionaries, came calling in the early seventeenth century. Most of the nation's villages were located within a forty-kilometre radius of Head of the Lake. The people were named "Neutral" by the French missionaries, because their nation occupied a neutral position between the tribes of the Iroquois Confederacy, who lived in the area south of Lake Erie, Lake Ontario and the Niagara River, and the Hurons, who lived farther north, beside Georgian Bay and Lake Huron.

Perhaps the Neutrals realized that they were no match for either of their neighbours, and tried to stay out of the way. Perhaps they were masters of compromise, who graciously bestowed that talent on the inhabitants of what later came to be called Canada. Or maybe they didn't have as much at stake as the Iroquois and Hurons, and were far enough removed from the sources of tension existing between those two tribes that they had no reason to get involved. Around this time the fur trade was moving west, above and below Lake Ontario. The Hurons supplied the French with furs, while the Iroquois worked with the Dutch. The Dutch supplied the Iroquois with a certain piece of equipment in numbers the French couldn't match. The Hurons were outgunned, and in the mid-seventeenth century the Iroquois invaded and rubbed them out as a nation.

The Attiwandaron, as the Neutrals called themselves, fared no better. An essay was written about the nation in one of the historical journals that sprang up in the late nineteenth century. By 1898, when the essay was published, the Six Nations of the Iroquois Confederacy had been occupying a reserve by the Grand River, thirty miles south of Head of the Lake, for more than one hundred years, far outside their ancestral territory and on land originally Neutral.

The author of the essay, Mary Rose Holden, who also signed herself "'Ka-rih-wen-ha-we,' Beaver Clan. Onondagas of the Six Nations," writes that the Attiwandaron sacrificed their neutrality, and thus their existence, over a matter of the heart, a statement which seems so typical of nineteenth-century romantic invention that it makes one wonder. The Attiwandaron society was matrilineal, as was the Iroquois. Women were the keepers of the fire. Attiwandaron neutrality meant that others could find safety from pursuers or enemies within the tribe's villages, which were recognized, she writes, as Cities of Refuge.

Into one such village came two Seneca warriors one day. The Seneca nation was part of the Iroquois Confederacy. The warriors were enjoying shelter when messengers arrived from a Mississauga village, claiming that the Senecas had recently murdered the son of their chief. The son evidently was the Attiwandaron Queen's lover. Overwhelmed with grief and vengeance, "she delivered the two Senecas up to be tortured and executed." This act so outraged the social order, and the Iroquois Confederacy, that it spelled the end of the Neutral nation. The Iroquois invaded, and the hearth fire of the Attiwandaron was extinguished.

> Indian tradition states that the heights and shores of our bay, stretching over the Beach, gave site to the final battle fought between the Neutrals and the Romans of the New World. To this day, the mention of Burlington Heights to some of the old chiefs on the Grand River Reserve (the Six Nations) brings the same gleam to the eye and expression to the carriage as the word "Waterloo" or "Trafalgar," gives to a loyal Briton.

The facts may have been a bit sketchy anyway, after two hundred and fifty years of oral retelling, but however much Mary Rose elaborated or embellished, and whatever the real story behind the event was, the claim by the Iroquois against their neighbours was the Neutrals' betrayal of their own neutrality, which, in the eyes of the Iroquois, justified the eradication of the Attiwandaron as a nation. "Neutral" had become, in effect, a contradiction in terms—the nation had cancelled itself out. During the days of the fur trade, however, neither the Iroquois nor any other native tribe needed much of a pretext to fight.

The next party of explorers to travel through the area, accompanied by Father Louis Hennepin, found none of the twenty-eight Neutral towns and villages documented by the earlier Jesuit party. The land was depopulated and uninhabited except by small groups of Mississauga natives who had drifted in from the east. It remained that way for the next one hundred years. Maybe the reason it is so hard to sense a native presence here is because for such a long period of time there simply wasn't one.

When the first settlers moved into the area at the end of the eighteenth century, they were moving into what was for the most part unoccupied territory. Those first settlers were refugees of the American Revolutionary War, many of them people who, like the Attiwandaron, had been run out of their homes and off land they had owned for generations. These were not willing immigrants arriving at their country of choice, for they were neither willing, nor was this a country. They were fleeing into an unsettled wilderness.

The British, for their part, had no plans at the time to colonize the land they controlled north of the thirteen states. They were fighting a war. The British fort at that time was still on what is now the American side of the Niagara River. They were not expecting company, but company started dropping by, almost from the moment the Revolution began.

> In 1776, there arrived at Fort Niagara, in a starving state, Mrs. Nellis, Mrs. Secord, Mrs. Young, Mrs. Buck, and Mrs. Bonnar, with thirty-one children, whom the circumstances of the rebellion had driven away.

The refugee families most often arrived without the husband and father, who was either fighting, in hiding, imprisoned, or dead. One of those thirty-one children, James Secord, was said to remember that

> as a child of three he had accompanied his mother in her flight through the wilderness, with four other homeless women and many children. After enduring frightful hard-

ships for nearly a month they finally arrived at Fort Niagara almost naked and starving.

It reads like the universal refugee experience, this fleeing to Neutral territory. As the Loyalist numbers grew, the British bought land across the river from the Mississaugas to grow food to feed them—and Lt. Thomas Cootes made off-duty hunting trips to the marsh at Head of the Lake. When it became obvious that these guests had nowhere else to go, and that more were coming, their hosts, in a series of treaties, bought more land up the Niagara Peninsula and farther into the unsettled province, so that these people, displaced through loyalty to the British crown, could begin over again.

The Loyalists' journey up the Peninsula was measured in the streams they crossed after crossing the Niagara: Two Mile Creek, Four Mile Creek, Six, Eight, Ten, Twelve Mile Creek, Fifteen, Sixteen Mile Creek, Twenty, Thirty, Forty Mile Creek. Some of the streams could be crossed on foot, others were deep and wide enough to require the floating of wagons and animals. Smaller, unnumbered streams ran in between. These people were only trying to get somewhere, to put some measureable distance between themselves and the ones who had driven them from home, and the names of these ribbons of running water were as descriptive and utilitarian as road directions, as the name, Head of the Lake. And, to my ear, just as musical. In some respects, these are as close as we come, here, to having place names that are rooted in the landscape and in our own relationship to the landscape.

THERE IS A STATUE in downtown Hamilton. It stands on the plot of ground that gave George Hamilton's envisioned site at Head of the Lake a leg up on the surrounding towns in its quest to become the area's judicial seat, in the generation after the Loyalist flight from the Revolutionary War. The land was donated by Hamilton for a courthouse and jail.

The statue faces north, in the direction that the young family it depicts is fleeing. The man's arm stretches over his daughter's head, his hand holding the slip of paper that grants land to his family on this side of the Niagara River. The four-year-old girl grips her father's coat with one hand and a doll with the other. The man's other arm is around the shoulder of his wife. The parents are caught mid-stride together, leaning forward slightly and peering intently ahead as if they can't see through the fog to what lies before them.

The woman has one hand placed on her stomach: thinking of the generations to come, if I read my sculptural symbology correctly. Her other hand reaches around the shoulders of her eight- or nine-year-old son, to pull him along. The son is reluctant, the only one of the four not facing forward. Half-turned to look back, he yearns not to flee but to stand and fight. In one arm he carries a shovel, in the other a hoe, wishing, perhaps, that they were firearms.

The statue's base is bronze-plaqued on all four sides, its message in upper case.

> NEITHER CONFISCATION OF THEIR PROPERTY,
> THE PITILESS PERSECUTION OF THEIR KINSMEN IN
> REVOLT, NOR THE CALLING CHAINS OF IMPRISONMENT
> COULD BREAK THEIR SPIRITS OR DIVORCE THEM
> FROM A LOYALTY ALMOST WITHOUT PARALLEL.

The statue was commissioned by descendants of a Loyalist

family—one of the future generations under the wife and mother's hand—and unveiled on Empire Day, May 24, 1929.

> ... TAKING UP ARMS FOR THE KING, THEY PASSED THROUGH ALL THE HORRORS OF CIVIL WAR AND BORE WHAT WAS WORSE THAN DEATH, THE HATRED OF THEIR FELLOW-COUNTRYMEN, AND, WHEN THE BATTLE WENT AGAINST THEM, SOUGHT NO COMPROMISE, BUT, FORSAKING EVERY POSSESSION EXCEPTING THEIR HONOUR, SET THEIR FACES TOWARD THE WILDERNESSES OF BRITISH NORTH AMERICA TO BEGIN, AMID UNTOLD HARDSHIPS, LIFE ANEW UNDER THE FLAG THEY REVERED.

... Taking their moral victory with them. Not to make light of their experience or to minimize the injustice and true misery the refugees faced, but these are pretty strong emotions to be casting in bronze one hundred and fifty years after the fact. As the orphan of a country on the other side of the ocean and, though born here, an adoptee of this one, I might think myself, by implication, far less noble than they, and left out, neither native nor deserving, unable to muster an equivalent emotion. And I'm certainly not the only one who could feel strong-armed to the margins by these plaques. I love the statue for its no-holds-barred declamation, but what gives? Did the Loyalists truly embrace their land of refuge, or were some of them only angrily, self-righteously resigned to being here, a century and a half later? Did the need to speak these words, after so many years, speak to the fact that they still did not feel a true belonging here, and in fact didn't want to?

THE LOYALISTS weren't the only ones sent packing by the

American Revolution. In the logic of the time and place, if you weren't for the revolution, you were against it. You didn't have to take sides in order to lose. Any group that refused, on principle, to fight, like the Mennonites and Quakers, was forced to leave as well. It amounted to a mass migration, and over the next couple of decades, even after the threat of expulsion was over, the movement continued, because by then the British had taken up the idea of colonization. Governor Simcoe was placing ads in the Philadelphia newspapers inviting settlers, offering free land with few strings attached. The wave of migration lasted until war broke out between the Americans and the British, again, in 1812.

But among the first migrants of the Revolutionary War period, who followed the five women and thirty-one children in walking to the Niagara River and stepping over into the now vacant lands of the Attiwandaron, were the tribes of the Iroquois Confederacy.

The Iroquois Confederacy did not practice neutrality during the Revolutionary War. Most of the Six Nations fought with and for the British. Toward the end of the war, in 1779, George Washington signed an order that both punished the natives and opened up valuable land to white settlement. The order sent General John Sullivan and five thousand American troops on one of the largest and most expensive campaigns of the war. Sullivan gathered his troops at the southern end of the Finger Lakes in New York State, the entrance to Iroquois lands, and systematically marched up between the lakes, destroying and burning each village and all crops as they went, driving the native people ahead of them.

Diaries kept by soldiers on this campaign describe the land they entered as a kind of paradise: cornstalks tall as a man on a horse, the ears of corn two feet long, and large, well-tended orchards, and storehouses full of food. The emptied land was handed over to the soldiers, who retired from active duty, and for fifty years this former home of the Iroquois Confederacy was the fruit and vegetable basket for the populated eastern part of the United States. By the end of this time, the farming soldiers had depleted the soil, and their grandchildren pulled up stakes, abandoning the farms and moving farther west, where more fresh land was being made available, in a fashion similar to that which had opened up the land they were leaving.

Mary and I used to drive through the lands of the Confederacy on our way to visit Mary's family in New Jersey, travelling between the long, narrow bodies of water laid out like large fingers on the landscape, past vineyards on gentle slopes, the small towns. A beautiful countryside, though we never could escape the bleak, unsettled atmosphere that hung like a grey cloud over the place. The drive made us both consistently uncomfortable and eager to be beyond it. When we learned about the soldiers' march, our sense seemed to be corroborated by history, and the trailers in the hillside trailer park we passed took on the appearance of derelict, miniature, metal longhouses.

Many of the Six Nations people who had been driven from the Finger Lakes did not survive their first winter along the south shore of Lake Ontario. Of those who did survive, many joined the movement of refugees west and across the Niagara, where the British government granted them a large reserve, stretching forty-eight kilometres on either side of the Grand River, from its source, north of Head of the Lake, to its mouth at Lake Erie. Almost immediately, the land was nibbled at and whittled away by land agents and settlers, but irony abounds: the Iroquois were granted land the British had recently purchased from a Mississauga tribe, who had more or less drifted into its ownership after the original occupants, the Attiwandaron, had been exterminated by the Iroquois themselves.

THE PATTERN OF NEUTRALITY, of this landscape taking in those who need refuge, repeats and focuses in on the Iroquois Bar.

In 1813, the American army crossed the Niagara River and marched up the corridor between the escarpment and the lake, forcing the people who'd been forced to flee a generation earlier to flee again, as homes were burned and crops destroyed by the advancing troops. The British army was encamped halfway to Head of the Lake, at the narrowest portion of the corridor, pinched between escarpment and lake, but when it became clear that there was no stopping the enemy march without reinforcement, they retreated to Burlington Heights on the Iroquois Bar.

The Heights was the end of the British defensive line. Surrounded by water on three sides, with only one point of access by land, it was their most easily defended fortification, as well as the most difficult for the enemy to attack effectively. It also offered little possibility of escape for the British, should the enemy actually take it.

The army was not alone in heading for the Heights. In the total upset of settlement life on the Niagara Peninsula, many of the burned-out and displaced settlers, war-wounded Indians and militiamen gathered there too, where they found food, shelter and medical attention. More people came when York was burned and occupied. Over a thousand native women and children fled to the Heights, including Tecumpease, sister of

Tecumseh, following the surprise retreat of the British army at Moraviantown, the subsequent rout of native warriors who stayed to fight, and Tecumseh's death.

The pull of the Heights during this period is what prompted the late-nineteenth-century writers to begin referring to it as a City of Refuge. The writers were echoing Attiwandaron neutrality, but they were also applying a biblical model to their home landscape, a model particularly tempting for them since, like the children of Israel, the settlers had entered the land and occupied it as successfully as if they were God's own chosen. The idea became part of the mythology these writers were trying to create. It was from this City of Refuge that seven hundred soldiers marched out on the night of June 5, 1813 to meet the thirty-five hundred American soldiers camped between the escarpment and the bay, and sent them running back to their homes across the river ... *ridding the peninsula of the invaders.*

It's hard to resist overplaying the theme. Some of the immigrants who began arriving over the Atlantic Ocean after the War of 1812 found a refuge they weren't looking for, under a rock on a point of land overlooking Cootes Paradise. Through the remainder of the century, the population beneath the ground grew, as more of the former British army encampment on the Iroquois Bar became burial ground. As the city expanded, its living inhabitants began to use the cemetery as retreat and refuge from urban density and the atmosphere of coal-burning, street-side industry. The area became a picnic and rendezvous place, a civic park, in a time when public parks did not yet exist.

Toward the close of the century, the first true park was opened, across the street from the cemetery, when Dundurn

Castle was purchased by the city. People appreciated being able to wander and enjoy the grounds more than the rooms of the mansion. During the same decade, others began to seek refuge in the small city of boathouses that was growing at the Desjardins canal cut.

The parks movement of the early twentieth century continued and institutionalized the theme of refuge. Cootes Paradise, a staging ground for bird migration, became a bird sanctuary in the twenties, and thus was saved from housing developments planned for its shoreline. Thomas B. McQuesten's beautification efforts, and the creation of the Royal Botanical Gardens, turned most of the Burlington Heights portion of the Bar into a place set aside to rest the weary soul.

Provided the weary soul can stand the uninterrupted sound of traffic.

Here we go again: in opposite directions, at equal speed. In the broader context of a culture that creates environments in places that make it undesirable or impossible to live in those places, Hamilton is something of a metaphor for the rest of the country. A century after "Ka-rih-wen-ha-we" wrote her essay, the stories that appear in the national press from the City of Refuge almost unfailingly reinforce a mythology of flight. Head of the Lake has become the pre-eminent place to fly away *from*.

One such recent story occurred when a warehouse in the industrial area of the city, near the bay, went up in flames. I noticed the black plume growing over the tops of buildings while out driving and went by the High Level Bridge for a better view. I wasn't alone. The sky was a cloudless, deep blue that early evening, setting the column of smoke in perfect, clear relief. A living mass of dense darkness growing in billows, blooming, a black rose in the sky. Awful beauty. A sight you hope to see only once in a lifetime.

The person standing next to me said, "There's only one thing that burns that way. Hydrocarbons. God Almighty."

A plastics recycler had gone up.

PERHAPS WHEN I STAND on the Iroquois Bar and yearn to sense a Native presence I'm already getting what I ask for. The presence is the place itself. This body of earth below my feet responds to our relationship with it by being itself. Within its escarpment embrace it holds our airborne contaminants, the exhausted smudge of industry, internal combustion and constant motion, for us to breathe in daily; and provides a still and clear blue evening so we can watch our worst fears rise like a prayer. A prayer attended by the firefighters who serve as priests of a kind, who themselves will later be offered up, to the small black clouds of cancer caused by this sacrifice.

You look down, because that's where the pain is coming from, and see it flow, water and blood.

I am not going to make a special case for where I live.

Great Spirit God Almighty, I thank you that I am not from here, but am here, an immigrant adoptee, a guest who stayed, a loyalist, a stone who came to land, to rest, on this bar of belonging.

I thank you for the long mound beneath my feet, the water on either side, for the trees that cover the hills that come to the water, the encircling arms of rock. I thank you for the wounds on this landscape, that I touch, that I share.

I thank you for the blindness that has let me see more deeply into this place. I thank you that I am pulled in opposite directions, at equal speed, by which I am made human.

I thank you for the path we are on, the path that leads nowhere.

THERE YOU HAVE IT: embarrassing behaviour in a public place. A little big man lifting praise into the winds that whip through the canal cut. I lean against the rail of the beloved bridge that spans the open laceration where flows the ancient, diverted stream, and it occurs to me that this is the selfsame rail Chic Collura climbed and jumped from, into the canal, far below. And lay himself down in the sand, and caught his wind, and picked himself up and walked home, with a little help from his friends.

What a marvelous nut-bar he must have been.

# Lay-by: lectio divina

(1:00–1:20: SATURDAY AFTERNOON; MID-JANUARY.
AT AN ALTERNATIVE LOCATION; IN-
DOORS, BUT SURROUNDED BY WINDOWS.)

A long train crosses the railway landfill embankment above where the Mercers' lived.

I will not make a special case for him, any more than I will make a special case for this landscape. He can make his own case.

Another long train crosses the embankment.

Trust the Catholics to know where to put their buildings. They find a focal point of the landscape and hallow it with cemetery, cathedral or convent. It's the old sacramental view, mostly foreign to us Protestants, excepting Presybterian Thomas B. McQ., with his bridge. Maybe there's hope. This convent for the Sisters of St. Joseph sits on the headland between two ravines that empty into the original, natural channel around the end of the Bar.

Nuns in retirement. Grandmother brides of Christ.

The sisters' chosen silence was broken when Chedoke highway was built, yet in this many-windowed room silence rules. From here the six lanes are a soundless blur I can barely make out through the trees. The long, rumbled work-chant of the train and the occasional start-up of the hot-water heater against the wall make the only real noise.

He's staring at me. I'm staring out the window of this chapel where I am parked in a chair, alone, him on the cross—small cross, small him—superimposed over the trees that grow from one of those two ravines. Which happens to be the ravine we walked through on our mild, mid-spring jaunt. The background is the entire landscape of Cootes Paradise and the Iroquois Bar.

Through the grey-brown upthrusting sticks of trees and branches, I can see the lumps and rumples of the shoreline hills and the long bulk of the Bar, shrouded in the past month's snow.

*Lectio. Meditatio. Oratio. Contemplatio.*

Why do I sit here and just wish to look? Like any other time that I find myself staring through a window, or sitting in the car at the lay-by. I'm supposed to be engaged in a four-step *lectio divina*, the spiritual reading of a passage of holy scripture. The others in the group who have come on this retreat have

each found their own private spot for this exercise: this chapel is mine. St. Joseph's opens its home to seekers and spiritual refugees of all stripes.

*Iroquois Bar, from Cootes Paradise*

My eyes climb up from the page, through the window, to feed on what's written outside, drink from the visual spring. And the eye tells the brain and the brain tells the body and the body feels a yen to move. Not linear movement, not toward or from, but movement here, in one spot, as the geese pass overhead, blending their chant with the train's.

My lectio divina, this landscape.

## St. Terra 

The train leaves the station at the centre of the earth
and enters the silence
of the one who is walking the tracks.

*Chunk.* Each step the walker takes
is a choice, a decision that punches through
the crust of ice that protects
the soft belly of snow
that perfects the shape of the landscape.

The alternative. *Chunk.* Is to tread
the tightrope rail itself, silver-brown
thread, over the gorgeous
new creation snow makes, that cheers
the crossing
        but balance is difficult
in boots, demands an alien
concentration

        and so the walker tramps
between the lines, piston feet
breaking surface, each footfall also
breaking silence with the place,
a sound the deep passage down
instantly absorbs,
        the imposed deliberation
of each step slowly
breaking through, prompting him to think

> *massage—*

and feel the earth relax.

He thinks to feel the earth relax
beneath this winter saunter of the tracks.
*Sant ter.* This pilgrimage
to the holy land of going nowhere
quick. *Saint Earth.* As though the feet
performed a kind of healing dance, like fingers up
and down a back, could coax the flow
of blood again, under the numbed wound—
the raised, halo scar of rail bed—

with nothing more asked
than to dare the simple intimacy of this touch.

The walker enters the giant, silent engine room
    of earth's centre,
stands back, waits
as the train whistles through the stations of snow.

# Selective Memory: *"I want to live here..."*

MY YOUNGEST DAUGHTER and her friend often accompany me on explorations of the Bar and surroundings, but my older daughter has come this time, too. We leave the car parked at Dundurn Castle. I recently noticed a path clinging to the sloped side of the Bar behind Dundurn. The path was part of a larger landscaping and path-making project of the 1930s, which covered much of the slope—a project I had been unaware of. Fragments of a scenic lookout still existed. I want to see how far the path still goes, and, if possible, lead the kids along it to the other side of the Desjardins canal, where I have promised them swans.

It takes only ten minutes or so to call them down from the cannon aimed over the bay—reminder of the War of 1812. They cling to the cannon's barrel as though it were the back of a horse, and crawl along the top until they can lean over the end and stare into the dark tunnel of its mouth. When they are finally done beating ordnance into playground equipment, we walk over to the edge of the slope where a break in the chain-link fence leads down a flight of steps to a flat deck of concrete: the old lookout, minus protective rail, and minus the view since trees have grown up in front.

Without the trees, this view could be a typical photo from the 1930s or 40s. One of those hand-tinted postcards of domestic scenic sights: the panoramas, the waterfalls and caves, magnetic hills, wooden bridges over tiny creeks, the path with wooden handrail beside a wall of rock. An implicit loyalty to the local. The greatest amount of pleasure squeezed out of the smallest natural details of home, and presented to the world. Come, see.

The path lies to our left, its opening likewise overgrown with foliage. We push through this green door into an area suddenly open and expansive, and at the same time push through the children's reluctance to enter at all. They haven't been too keen to follow: only the promise of swans has kept them willing. But now they proceed to be enthralled.

The path is no more than a narrow horizontal line between a vertical wall on the left and a steep slope on the right, and part of the thrill is the sheer danger. Soon the kids' hands are all over and into the wall. They've never seen anything like it. It's built in layers, like bricks or concrete blocks would be, but isn't flat like the wall of a building: the layers are set-back, slanted, or they stick out from the ones above and below. Each layer is made of something different from the others. The girls pick at the small round stones of one loosely-packed layer, then dig into the cool damp sand of another, or try to bang off tennis-ball size stones from a mortared-together layer.

The mortared layers are harder than the others and often project further out from the wall. There are places where the wall beneath is undercut, or hollowed out, and forms a small cave—the kind of place where a rattlesnake might have wanted to curl during the days when George and Al were walking to Granny Mercer's. There are also places where the slope on our right is undercut and the path becomes a balcony to an audience of trees, where the children take turns standing, making speeches, declaring themselves victorious and very pleased.

We walk along, slowly, thoroughly engrossed, preoccupied with our surroundings, enchanted, until we reach a spot, halfway to the High Level, where the path has been obliterated by the collapse of the wall. The harder layer has been undercut too deeply, could no longer support itself and the weight above—the Niagara Gorge effect. We have to climb up, over the rubble, and it isn't a simple or safe business, but by now the girls are so exhilarated they are ready to tackle anything. One takes the lead, the others follow. They give each other hand-in-hand pulls, hand-on-heel pushes, while I take up the rear to break any falls. Emerging through the leaves at the top, we leave the cool dampness of the many stones' solitude and walk into a wall of sudden heat and humidity, and are public again.

Yet nothing intrudes on the stillness we've taken up with us from the path. The traffic on York Boulevard, thirty metres away across the grass sward, though heavy, remains remarkably subdued, obeisant. We keep as far away from the road as possible, following another narrow path between a chain-link fence and the top edge of our wall, and come to a place where the path turns and begins to go down the side of the Heights toward the Desjardins canal. It's an old roadbed, a remnant, I tell them as we walk. It leads to a bridge that no longer exists, though the stone stumps that supported the bridge are still standing on either side of the canal. Three teenage boys are fishing from one of the stumps.

There's a story behind that missing bridge. There's a story behind each of the six that span the canal. The effect in the confined area of the cut is a bit overwhelming: the round, high shoulders of the cut, the number and size of the bridges that connect the shoulders, the green width of the canal that the bridges span. I decide not to tell my three companions about the wild flinging-apart of the first suspension bridge. Or about the one built to replace it, the Bridge of Sighs as it was nicknamed, built so poorly it was said even dogs wouldn't cross. As we step onto the railway bridge, I decide not to mention the train that broke its axle and crashed through the bridge into the canal, or tell them that, afterward, trains would stop to allow anyone who wished to walk across to do so, as we are doing. It's enough to concentrate on each step we take, as those crash-conscious riders did a century and a half ago, tie by tie, the water of the canal far below and glittering through the slits.

On the other side, we slide down a steep slope to the shore. The shoreline forms a little finger here, a spit of land that extends into the bay and then runs parallel to the side of the Bar, creating its own little bay of marsh and bulrushes. The swans nest at the finger's tip. I know about the swans from a friend who rides past in the commuter train each day.

We follow a shoreline path past a firepit on the beach, past the windblown and floating debris caught on rock, in branches, past the water-exposed roots of willow trees, walking through bush and bullrush. I *do* tell about the former boathouse community, but there's not one clue, not a single shred of evidence to indicate that houses once stood, that people lived and children played here. A man and a woman sit on tree stumps, their fishing poles bent over the bay like the antennae of a large insect. They turn their heads to us and stare, and the man flicks the tail-end of a still-lit, proprietorial cigarette into the bay as we pass by. We hear its quick *fssst* in the water. The kids are silently appalled.

The finger of shoreline curls in on itself and is thick with bulrushes at its tip, but the path pushes through and we manage to get quite close to the nest. Two swans patrol the coast, keeping a close eye. The nearer we get to their home the more difficult the going becomes, and we step gingerly on flattened, floating bulrushes because solid ground has diminished to nothing. *We're walking on water*, one of the girls says. But then we're sinking and have to turn back without having seen either eggs or little ones.

We retreat to a black willow we'd had to climb over to get to the area of the nest. The tree must have received a double blow. It is tipped-over, with roots exposed, and also has its trunk cracked in half over the path. The girls debrief as they explore, investigate. Under the horizontal trunk and in the lee of the exposed root ball, someone has arranged rocks around a firepit. Along with the usual shards and discards of plastic and paper, a few empty cans litter the ground, baked beans, and a water-logged Bible.

The two younger girls pretend this is home. Water quietly laps the sand at the root ball, the swans still patrol the coast, and it seems perfectly plausible that a person would choose to make this their refuge, retreat. No sound of traffic filters through, and it's surprisingly far removed from the world. The girls climb under and over the barrel of the fallen trunk, and stand on top to preach loudly against the fishing butt-flickers. A moment of quiet meditation settles on them, mid-rant, and one says,

"I want to live here."

A moment later the other replies, "Me too."

They climb down and huddle by the firepit, fixing dinner. I didn't know until this moment that this is exactly what I've wanted to hear them say.

It takes only twice as long to call them out from under the trunk as it did to call them down from atop the cannon. The offending fisher-couple is still connected by two thin filaments to the water. We climb the path to the tracks and watch a passel of teens on two-wheelers spit down from the higher railway bridge onto the two teens still fishing from the old bridge stump. Following the tracks back instead of the path, we begin collecting.

First, it's an unbroken glass insulator unscrewed from the arms of a hydro pole which has been snapped in half like a matchstick and is lying on the ground. This whole line of poles is mysteriously snapped in half and prone.

Then a rusty, eight-inch bolt and nut. And another piece of metal, unidentifiable but interestingly shaped.

Following the tracks is hotter and more humid than was walking the path. Pants sag from the weight in our pockets as we step tie to tie. I look back often, remembering too vividly a train that once came upon me from behind, and almost overtook me, in complete silence.

The oldest has told the two younger girls that you can "feel" a train coming by putting your ear to the track. The friend dearly desires the experience, while my daughter is not so sure. The first is rewarded when her ear feels the slow-moving freight train that then emerges into view at the far end of the Iroquois Bar. She is also the only one carrying coins. I've told them what we did with pennies as kids, and she now methodically removes, a copper at a time, one for each of us from the pack buckled around her waist, dispensing precious goods from her personal, small horde.

Just as methodically, our pennies are placed on the rail. The train bears down, growing enormous in size and sound. We run to take cover beside a small railway shack that's standing in the ditch—standing remarkably close to where the Beasleys' original log home stood, in fact. We wave to the engineer, who blows his horn, making the impossibly momentous mass of brown steel even larger as it rolls by, more size than sound, completely subduing our senses.

The world returns after the train's passing, but only two pennies survive, the other two having disappeared into the gravel bed of the tracks. One of the survivors is destined for the shelf at home, along with the other things we've collected, the "valuable junk." Tired and exhilarated by the two-hour expedition, we climb the slope through the trees to the castle parking lot. Halfway up, the girls discover a chrome kitchen chair, with plastic upholstery. They right it, wipe it clean with leaves, and while the other two stand and attend, each takes her turn to sit incongruously among the trunks and greenery.

A final push. We stagger to the top. And take the Heights.

# MacNab's Favour

WHEN PEOPLE FROM OTHER LANDS come calling, we take them to Dundurn Castle. Showing Dundurn to guests, particularly to guests from over the Atlantic, taxes the spirit, however, because invariably they feel called upon to comment. "You call this a castle? In Europe we have *real* castles." Between the dream and the reality, between word and meaning, stand the literalists.

They're right, of course. Dundurn is no more a castle than the Niagara Escarpment running through Hamilton is a mountain. It has no turret, no drawbridge, no moat, no metre-thick walls, no dungeon, no hangman, no blood marks on stone. It *does* have an indoor bowling alley, a dovecote, a basement brewery, a differently-toned servant's bell for each room, the first flush toilet in the land, numerous other nineteenth-century innovations in domestic comfort, and countless nooks and crannies.

By the time the guide, dressed in period wear, bows or curtsies goodbye, our guests are usually won over by the place, despite the troublesome misnomer. For all its size, the house feels neither vast nor cold. Dundurn is liveable. Its castleness is of the "A man's home is his ..." variety—if you'll pardon the patriarchy. Which can hardly be said for those stone edifices back in the European homeland.

Among the features the guide points out are Dundurn's walls within walls. The original architect was instructed to incorporate into his design a house already standing on the spot where the new one was to be built. That house was the two-storey, Loyalist-style brick home of Richard and Henrietta Beasley—their second home, atop the Iroquois Bar rather than beside the bay. The new owner wished to contain and ennoble the past within the present: to remember, not replace or obliterate. Allan MacNab envisioned an estate that bespoke continuity within the landscape, reflected permanence and succession. It suited his proprietorial fancy, as well as his ambitions, to have the Beasley brick subsumed into his country seat.

Given his client's other requirements for the building, the architect, Robert Wetherell, had his work cut out for him in terms of melding old with new. He accomplished the task deftly. Dundurn is patterned on the large, comfortable farmhouses of Tuscany, a villa in a style called Regency Italianate. It and the Beasleys' home are two utterly different structures, but if you know what you're looking for—door placement, window layout, room arrangement—the previous house is there both in body and in spirit. Dundurn Castle is one of the oldest buildings in the city, and the fact that the material ghost of a building even older is contained within it, a doll within a doll, takes it even further back in time, to the beginning of settlement life at Head of the Lake.

Part of the MacNab lore centres around the troublesome "castle." He began building in 1832, and the house was finished three years later, but the adding and renovating continued, on and off, into the 1850s. The story has MacNab peering over the visiting tax assessor's shoulder during the final renovations of 1854, instructing him to append the word to a property listing which until then had read simply "Dundurn". The man's pride had reached the very heights. He was due for a fall.

These final renovations, and the addition of a portico over the front door, were being done in preparation for the marriage of his daughter, Sophia, and by this time the self-made man of privilege *had* reached a personal height. Sir Allan Napier MacNab had recently been chosen as the first Prime Minister of a newly united Upper and Lower Canada. He'd served as his area's member of parliament already for twenty years, and Speaker of the House for almost as many. Knighthood had come in 1838, in recognition of MacNab's military service in the Rebellion of 1837. In addition, this lawyer, land-owner and developer was a successful railway promoter, his greatest achievement having reached fruition on January 19 of that same year, 1854, when, in spite of much controversy and criticism, the Great Western rolled into town along the bay shore of the Iroquois Bar, passing under his bedroom window at Dundurn—where he had wanted, and fought, to have it go.

On the evening of the train's arrival, however, Sir Allan *could* only watch from his bedroom window. He observed the hoopla and heard the twenty-one gun salute fired in his honour, his name shouted and cheered by the crowd below, but wasn't able to participate in the celebrations because he was laid up with gout, a disease often triggered by stress. The odd little irony of this physical incapacitation at the height of his personal achievement, as the train steams by, larger than life, serves almost as a premonition of the slowing down of MacNab's own forward motion. A slowing down that brakes to a halt not long after Sophia's marriage.

SOPHIA MACNAB was born the same year the work began on Dundurn. Her father had initiated the purchase of the Beasleys' property before her birth in July 1832, but the cholera epidemic that hit the city in August of that year scared him off.

I picture him standing with Robert Wetherell by the road in front of the Beasley house as the carts start to roll past carrying the new immigrants to the converted British army barracks farther down the road on Burlington Heights, or their coffins to the mass graves there. He is giving Wetherell his expansive vision of Dundurn and the Heights, pointing and gesturing as the dust from the carts settles on their hats and on the Beasleys' windowsills, because, in a style that the Loyalists brought with them from their American home, the road runs between the house and its barn.

MacNab backed away from the purchase that summer, but in November one of the buildings he owned downtown burned to the ground, while his own home suffered damage from the fire and needed extensive repair. The same day, he signed an agreement to buy the Beasleys' home, and almost immediately petitioned the city to have York Road rerouted around his new property.

Twenty-two years later, he stands before his realized dream, Dundurn, again pointing and gesturing, this time for the edification and instruction of the latest in a line of architects, Frederick Rastrick (Wetherell died in 1846). The two men discuss the addition of a portico, which will enhance the front entrance, and shelter guests arriving for Sophia's marriage. Sir Allan is thinking, *castle*. The carts that meanwhile carry the diseased, dying or deceased victims of a second cholera epidemic cannot be seen through the six-foot-high fence that surrounds the estate, nor, from this distance, are they heard. The tax assessor stops by to discuss the proposed improvements.

The juxtapositions seem almost biblical: the start and completion of a home that is representative of landed belonging, lasting achievement and lineage, coinciding with the birth and marriage of the child who is not an heir, as carts, bearing unnumbered immigrants ravaged by disease, rattle by.

But between the dream of Dundurn and its final reality, other mitigating events also occurred.

When MacNab arrived in Hamilton in the 1820s, he was already a widower with two small children. One of those children, his heir, Robert Allan, died in a shooting accident at the age of twelve. Robert was the first to be buried in the small, walled Dundurn cemetery, Inchbuie, where MacNab's first wife was then re-interred. MacNab's first daughter by Mary Stuart, his second wife, died shortly after birth. A new heir, Napier MacNab, was born to MacNab's brother but died one month later. Then that brother died; then MacNab's father; and in 1846, Mary Stuart, the mother of Sophia, succumbed to a lengthy illness. In the constant push and pull of joy and sorrow, success and failure, life and death, MacNab's experience may not have been uncommon to the time. Still, this part of his story helps to humanize someone who is often cast as having gotten what he deserved in his fall from the heights.

In the end, most of what MacNab worked so long to

get was taken away. A year after Sophia's marriage, he was forced out of the role of Prime Minister. Not long after, he resigned his seat in the House. His second daughter married. Both daughters and husbands relocated—to England and Australia—and Dundurn Castle, the family seat and home, suddenly stood virtually empty. In November of 1861 Sir Allan set sail to visit Sophia and do research into the MacNab line in Scotland, but lost all his personal and family papers in a shipwreck on the St. Lawrence River. He died at Dundurn, broken, half a year later.

Almost immediately the fighting began. Catholics and Protestants wrangled over his immortal soul, and his body, both claiming deathbed utterances that supported their side. Meanwhile, the newspapers chipped away at MacNab's public stature. They'd been doing some preliminary work already, with smaller implements, but now they went at it with sledges. MacNab's sister-in-law, Sophia Stuart, became executor and put Dundurn's contents and furnishings up for sale at auction. She then moved to Australia, and for four years Dundurn Castle stood vacant.

Given the dreams of legacy it was built to substantiate, one might be tempted to call the place MacNab's Folly, as the family line at Dundurn ended where it began, with Sir Allan himself. But for the house. Dundurn is a success in every way MacNab envisioned, in terms of how it works within its setting. Long after his departure, it stands as integral to the landscape and life here as pebble and cobble, tree and we.

And the lore of how the house came to be called Castle? The tour guide smiled and nodded during our last visit-with-guests as the tale was rehearsed, then informed us that her own recent research into the tax rolls of the time turned up no evidence of the infamous name-change. However the word came to be appended to the name Dundurn, the fact that it happened in this city suggests MacNab's home may have become his Castle in the same way the Niagara Escarpment became a Mountain. To most of the people who lived here it may just as well have been one—that's how likely it was they would ever set foot inside. Compared to their own humble abodes, that's exactly how Dundurn looked: like a castle.

Or perhaps people were taking a jab at McNab's pretensions.

Or maybe Sophia Stuart coined it, as she composed the real estate advertisements for Dundurn after the laird's death. "This is not just a house, but ...."

YOU AMBLE ABOUT THE HOME with your fellow guests. Sometimes the tour begins in the warren of basement rooms where the servants worked and ate and slept, where the main kitchen was, and where the tour guide will point out an exposed portion of the wall-within-the-wall, the foundation of the Beasleys' house. Or it may begin on the main floor, where, in the front hallway, you'll stand before a large Robert Whale painting of the city of Hamilton as seen from the escarpment top in 1854—that year, again—a work emblematic of the place in all its natural, inhabited beauty. You can see from the painting how someone might get the idea for a villa fashioned after the ones in the Tuscany countryside. The small brush stroke in the top left corner is Dundurn.

Or you may climb the servants' staircase and begin on the second floor, where, on an unguided but sanctioned solo tour, I once opened a closet door and discovered another, more intimate, material ghost, a framed sampler, embroidered by one of Richard and Henrietta Beasley's daughters in 1811, when the family still lived in the house that's now within the walls of Dundurn.

Depending on the disposition of your guide, the story may emphasize the oppression of the workers, who maintained the daily routine of the ruling class, their ablutions, the seven daily meals. You'll hear about the eleven-year-old girl who spent her entire sixteen-hour day washing dishes in the basement. The ten-year-old boy who, with the other male servants, slept in the loft of the stable, and performed the early morning task of emptying his master and mistress's chamber pots, and carrying boiling water in pails up two flights of stairs for their baths. The cook, ruler of the serving class, with her small private room with its window onto the basement hallway, to keep an eye on things, her daily ration of beer.

The story may focus on the lives of the owners, with details provided courtesy of the diary kept by Sophia MacNab, when she was thirteen. She kept the diary for less than a year, the year of her mother's death, but it has proven invaluable in giving a picture of daily life at Dundurn. You'll see the room where the two MacNab daughters were taught by their tutor, the sickroom of Mary Stuart, Sophia's mother, the bedroom and window through which the laird looked down upon his steaming achievement beside the bay, and the small upholstered bench that supported his gouty limb.

The baggage car of the history train remains virtually sealed on most tours, however, and not a great deal of background is given on the man whose house you're in: not a lot offered on the strange and typical confluence in him of ambition and accomplishment, rise and fall, that had such a shaping effect on the city and its sense of self—as well as on a significant part of its geography. This city's son, or father, Sir Allan Napier MacNab, is not the military, national or civic hero today that he was once. We've been of two minds about the man since the day he died, and had been for some time before that, and have never truly made our peace with him.

SOPHIA STUART, Sir Allan's sister-in-law, eventually leased Dundurn as an asylum for deaf and dumb children. Given her other actions in relation to the place, her choice of tenants seems almost a comment on her brother-in-law who, for all his ambition, failed even to produce an heir. She later sold the building to a syndicate said to have plans to turn Dundurn into a spa, but nothing more was heard of these plans.

In 1872, Donald and Mary Ameilia MacInnes purchased the castle and, together with their six children, turned Dundurn into a family residence again. The couple had previously owned George Hamilton's home, Bellevue. They tried to locate and acquire the original furniture for Dundurn, without much success. They improved and renovated, added a bowling alley. Dundurn remained a private home—it's hard to remember now that it isn't one, and hasn't been for over one hundred years—until just before the turn of the century. The last family event to take place in Dundurn was the marriage of the MacInness's daughter, in 1895.

MacInnes sought for a number of years to have the city purchase the castle and grounds, and four years after the wedding the city finally did. Much hoopla—in the form of parades, fireworks, visiting dignitaries from far and wide, military shows, cannons fired into the air, speeches—accompanied Dundurn's opening as a park. Housing and industry lived side by side in Hamilton, as they did in most cities at the time, and public parkland was a new concept. The opening-up of a private estate, previously fenced, for the benefit of the general populace, was even more novel. Over time, various attractions were added, such as a gazebo/bandshell, a small zoo and an aviary, while the house itself became a museum—home to the hodgepodge collection of whatever people chose to donate, from knick-knacks to formal wear—that one curator called "Hamilton's attic."

In 1967, Dundurn Castle became the city's Centennial Project, and the long process of restoring it as a family residence began. Furnishings and decorations are now organized around a specific year, 1855, Sophia's wedding year. Gardens and grounds are being reconstructed. Archaeological digs take place on the grounds and in the basement of the castle itself. Researchers in the guise of house servants, tour guides, delve into property tax rolls, deeper arcana. Dundurn is as fawned over now as it was during MacNab's and MacInnes's times.

THERE'S A PLEASING SYMMETRY in the fact that the three who arguably had the greatest effect on the city and the city's relationship to its geography all lived on or beside this Iroquois Bar I've gone on about: George Hamilton, in Bellevue, where the Bar meets the Niagara Escarpment, in the shadow of the rock wall that runs through the city; Thomas B. McQuesten, in Whitehern, in the heart of the settlement, at the base of the Bar; Allan MacNab, in Dundurn Castle, at the point where the Bar leaves the raised bed of the former glacial lake and stretches across the water. Where, on his first time journeying to town along York Road, he took in the three-hundred-and-sixty-degree view of bay and marsh, escarpment and trees, and came upon the Beasleys' house, with its prospect over the bay, and thought, *Here* ...

Part of me can hardly believe that the Iroquois Bar still exists, or Burlington Heights, given all that has happened to the urban landscape over the years. I feel the same about Dundurn Castle, and Whitehern. Whitehern came to the city directly from the family who had lived in it for a century, but Dundurn's history offered enough oppportunities for it to go the way of so many other older buildings in the city, including the home of Hamilton's founder. Why wasn't Dundurn brought down, dismantled? Many other nineteenth-century buildings suffered that fate. They still do. Why wasn't its property divided into lots and built upon? Its presence seems as much a dream as when MacNab first envisioned it.

Dundurn is oriented to face those leaving the city on the main road out, York Boulevard—the road to York, now Toronto—rather than those entering. Dundurn's formal address is made to those who dwell *here*. We wait at the traffic lights. On green, we thread the needle between this standing memorial to one man's pride of place, his ambition and accomplishment, and the cemetery's memorial to many, to all the forebears and ancestors who are part of the city's historical and physical landscape, the generations laid among the stones that support and carry us as we travel between neighbour and stranger, family and community, achievement and anonymity, moving over and across the water.

It's we who are Allan MacNab's extended, adoptive family—the great percentage of us immigrants, like those who were carted past his home, alive or dead; or their survivors; or the more recent arrivals, guests who pull in to the parking lot to exercise the privilege of wandering through the place as though we owned it. Or we've lived on a nearby street since Sophia MacNab was a toddler. A friend purchased a house in the neighbourhood around the castle after learning it had been in one family, all of whose fathers and sons were gardeners at Dundurn, since the day the gardens were first laid out. Continuity within the landscape: landed gentry, of the populist kind.

The man, MacNab, did us a favour.

# Two Hundred Years to the Day

WE DOUBLE-CHECK the date on the bronze plaque on the big rock beside the parking lot.

> ON THIS SITE IN 1785 WAS ERECTED
> ONE OF THE FIRST LOG HOUSES
> IN THIS DISTRICT BY LOYALIST PIONEER
> COL. RICHARD BEASLEY WHO ON
> JUNE 11TH AND 12TH 1796
> HERE ENTERTAINED
> LIEUT. COLONEL JOHN GRAVES SIMCOE
> THE FIRST LIEUTENANT-GOVERNOR OF
> UPPER CANADA AND MRS. SIMCOE.

The checking is mere formality. Our dinner party has been planned in advance to fall on the same day, two hundred years later, that the King of England's governing representative to Upper Canada, together with his wife, paid a visit to one of the first, if not *the* first, settler families at Head of the Lake. And stayed for dinner.

Mary and I will play host couple for this commemorative

repast. She, landed immigrant to Canada, soon-to-be citizen, born and raised in the state of New Jersey, original home to many Loyalists, is Henrietta Beasley. I, born in a town beside the Saint Lawrence River, of parents born and raised in Friesland, the Netherlands, am her husband, Richard. We met one day while I was out riding in an area of Cootes Paradise called Beasley's Hollow, which Chedoke highway runs through now, and came upon the frightened young Miss Springer, who had been seized and carried off by natives. I was honoured to be her rescuer.

Friends Bernadette and Wes are the diarist Lady Elizabeth and Lieutenant-Governor John Graves Simcoe. Bernadette, of the ravine hike, is Kentuckian; descendant of the Big Knives who fought, with unbridled passion, for the losing side, and crossed the Niagara River on that ill-fated invasion of the Peninsula, during the War of 1812: immigrant, now citizen. Wes, the only full-blooded Canadian in our group: born in the Yukon, raised on the prairies, educated in the Maritimes, now resident of Upper Canada.

Our loyalties, truly, are neither racial nor national, but lie in friendship and this casual ritual of eating together without walls.

> When we had near crossed the Bay Beasley house became a very pretty object. We landed at it and walked up the hill ...

Land-based creatures that we are, we have chosen to approach the site of Beasley house on foot rather than over water. Behind the large, standing rock by the parking lot of Dundurn Castle, the land falls abruptly away into the ravine,

*Two Hundred Years to the Day*

at the bottom of which the Beasleys lived, on the shoreline of the bay. We walk down the hill carrying our picnic supplies, and at the bottom pass an archaelogical dig: a perfectly squared hole, measuring a metre wide by two metres long, and one metre deep. A washout of the slope above has cut a deep gash in the side of the ravine, a few trees, large and small, are toppled, and a portion of the trench has been filled by the miniature avalanche of earth.

We search for a clearing in the sumach. Sumach usually indicates a disturbed site, though to my knowledge the only recent disturbances are these digs. Perhaps the sumach signifies the ongoing, eternal disturbance that the Heights, the Bar, and all the sacred earth is subject to, as the price for having creatures such as us aboard.

We select a site, spread a blanket for our spread of food, and settle in for a repast that includes tuna salad substituting for the salmon the Simcoes purchased from natives fishing on the bay, smoked turkey slices standing in for their wild turkey, fresh buns, salad, and wine. A number of black walnut trees are growing at the bottom of the ravine, among the sumach. Some of the first settlers who crossed the Niagara River followed what was called the trail of the black walnut. They were pacifists, Plain Folk, whose earlier experience of pioneering, of finding and selecting the choicest land, gave them knowledge that the tree grew on fertile limestone soil.

Disturbance and fertility together, roots intertwining.

The ravine *is* disturbed, of course. Much of it is now filled-in, for one thing. Beasley himself cut a narrow road and landfilled portions of the ravine to make getting from his wharf to the top of the ravine easier. One of his storehouses stood at the top lip, with a basement door that opened onto the cart path.

Part of the path, a road remnant, is still visible, and walkable; a dig is planned, I've learned, to see if any valuable junk once fell unnoticed from wagon or person, two hundred years ago.

Between our party and the bay lies Sir Allan's pride and joy, the railway. It would be easier to think well of his accomplishment if only the single track that he looked upon from his bedroom window separated us from the water, rather than an entire marshalling yard's expanse of tracks, laid side by side across this substantial swath of landfill. We're quite a distance from the current shoreline, though close to where we sit, amazingly, a short stretch of the old shoreline, where the Simcoes landed their canoe, still exists, complete with a small patch of water and bulrushes.

My one square inch, not clawed, raked, dug or filled, though somewhat debris-strewn. Thank you, thank you, thank you.

Meanwhile, a loud quartet of birds hidden somewhere in sumach and walnut entertains us. We know it's a quartet because it finally distracts us sufficiently with its music that we pay closer attention. As we open the basket and uncork the wine it suddenly becomes clear to us who those four in the branches are. Two hundred years later, they have returned to commend the occasion.

> I was so pleased with this place that the Gov. stay'd & dined at Beasley's.

Love is difficult. The practice of love is complex, contradictory and embattled. If it is possible to maintain a sense of wonder, to entertain serendipity and enjoy romance within the tangled garden of our urban habitation, today, after two hundred years, I'm all for it.

It's easy enough to fantasize a one-to-one relation with a pristine, natural environment while carrying shelter and supplies into the wilderness, knowing your stay is time-limited, and your return to the creature comforts immanent—those very comforts that make possible this incursion into the less populated, the more wild. Perhaps the desire to leave the city and head to the hills or lakes is the desire to escape from a romance suffering from too much history, in which the partners are having difficulty seeing each other as individuals any longer, much less as lovers. In the wilderness there's a new landscape to romance, a new partner, who briefly allows you to forget the one back home, the one who carries the signs of experience on his or her body, the highly unromantic scars of age, ailment, abuse.

The habited landscape of this mid-sized city and surrounding countryside understands me, its brokenness mirrors my own. This long-term intimacy with the nature of where I live is both a choice I've made, and a daily decision. Feelings of wanting to stay, and of dearly desiring to leave, come and go, like water, like the wave-laid twelve pebbles, twelve syllables, that organized themselves on the beach of my mind.

*I am attached to a piece of geography.*

The bundle of deadfall strapped to my back grows larger all the time with the lost, tossed and broken objects, stories picked up from beside the roads, paths and road remnants that have led to where this picnic takes place tonight. Yet the bundle travels lightly. The snapped branches offer up a small fire to brown our marshmallow dessert.

I keep returning to the two couples who dined together one evening two hundred years ago because their repast took place in the period of the first flush of romance between people and this place. I am descended from, and make my claim on them. They are Grandmother and Grandfather: the couple who lived here and opened their door, offering hospitality, and the couple who came calling. Somewhere in this moment between host and guest is the beginning of community, embodied later as city. Remembering their evening together is a way of claiming a little bit of that original landscape, too.

Having *stay'd* & *dined* on our simple meal, we clean, pack, and hike back up the hill.

> The hill is quite like a park, fine turf with large Oak trees dispersed but no underwood ...

It is still quite like a park, with mown lawn, middle-aged maple, locust, catalpa, oak trees, and no underwood. We stroll along the edge of the Bar that faces the bay, as the weather that has been idly threatening all evening begins to make good. The shades of grey above us become one shade. The diminishing light of day, the low clouds, build into a solid wall of darkness that advances from the east, over the bay. Already the Skyway Bridge at the lake-end of the bay is invisible, cloaked.

The thunder starts first, then lightning. With each jagged splitting of the sky Mrs. Beasley involuntarily squeezes my hand. The drumming that follows grows closer, crazier, each time. As we near the High Level Bridge, it is possible to watch the grey mass moving low over the surface of the water, with incredible speed, an invasion. When it reaches shore, we are soaked through instantly, the deluge catching us just as we cross the bridge over the canal. A real meeting place, this. We may as well be swimming.

The Governor is prepared. He has taken along our plastic groundsheet. We each gamely take a corner and hold it as a canopy over our heads, our coach-and-four. But the same wind that flung the suspension bridge apart so many years ago lifts the sheet from underneath and flings it about so wildly that it becomes clear two people could better control it than four, and Mrs. Beasley and I insist the Simcoes take full advantage of its protection for themselves, while she and I offer ourselves fully to the elements.

> We walked two miles on this Park, which is quite natural, for there are no settlements near it ...

Once past the bridge, we cross York Boulevard to the Cootes Paradise side. The rain drives up at us from the pavement almost as violently as it is driving down. We reach the area of the cholera stone, walk down the steps to the small reflecting pool that's tucked among the trees. People once stopped at the lay-by to pause in restorative reflection, contemplation, meditation, but they did so in an era of fewer wheels and lower speed limits. The long, rectangular, shallow basin has been minimally maintained for years, feels decidedly abandoned, and not many stop here now, not for reasons of reflection, at least. I've never actually seen water in the pool.

Enough rain has fallen and collected in the pool that the reflection from a street light is shining on the hyperactive surface of the water. We can't see our faces in all the disturbance, though, and hardly pause. Shouting conversation, we climb the steps and walk more slowly back to the car through the unrelenting downfall. Only our underwear manages to stay somewhat dry, at the waistband.

Back home, Mrs. Beasley and I change into dry clothing, and offer the Simcoes our bathrobes to wear as their clothes toss about in the dryer. The loud banging from the basement turns out to be the Governor's Swiss Army knife, which he'd left in his trouser pocket. Always prepared. The knife would fit well on the shelf of selective memories I've been showing them.

> ... the country appears to be more fit for the reception of inhabitants than any part of the province I have seen ...

Now is the moment. I have long wanted to ask if the story is true or apocryphal: during the Simcoes' visit, did the Governor inquire into purchasing the Beasley place in order to turn it into a townsite? If so, did Beasley really set a figure so high that negotiations stopped before they started? And if he did set so high a price, was he a shameless real estate speculator, or had he and Henrietta, after only a few years, already come to value the place so highly that its worth was inestimable, they really didn't want to sell for any amount?

Forty years after dinner with the Simcoes, the Beasleys are forced to sell their property on the Heights for financial reasons. The next owner works to build and create the home and country seat of landed gentry, but the line he imagines stretching into the future ends with him. Meanwhile, the Beasleys' fall from landed grace gives the family roots and branches, *large Oak trees dispersed*, that ramify through the stones and soil and air of Head of the Lake.

But I am Richard tonight, so whom shall I ask?

It has been a wonderful evening, beyond expectation. Our guests sit comfortably on our sofa, in our bathrobes, two hundred years after the fact. Our guests look, well, at home in our castle made of bricks that are made from the red clay shale that lies exposed in the walls of the northshore ravines of Cootes Paradise; our home made from the soil of home, or better, our home made from the stuff we are made of.

Slyly, roles reverse. We begin to receive broad hints that it may be time for us to make ourselves scarce, to hit the road.

Just who is guest and who host in this relationship to the earth we share with others of our regenerative species? I am so pleased with this place, despite the hurt and history. This dwelling, where I feel myself both landed gentry and honoured guest. Where the landscape continually shifts, stirs and reveals something inestimable of itself, lifts another stone from its Bar, relates the story, offers up another item to place on the shelf, and invites me to consider all that it has as my own.

Bowing good night as the door closes, I pledge to return the favour.

# Selected Bibliography

*The Diary of Mrs. John Graves Simcoe, wife of the first Lieutenant-Governor of the province of Upper Canada, 1792-6, with notes and a biography by J. Ross Robertson, and 237 illustrations, including 90 reproductions of interesting sketches made by Mrs. Simcoe;* Ontario Pub. Co., Toronto; 1934.

*The Sleeping Lord, and other fragments,* by David Jones; Faber and Faber, London; 1974.

*Thomas Baker McQuesten: Public Works, Politics and Imagination,* by John C. Best; Corinth Press, Hamilton; 1991.

*New and Collected Poems,* by Richard Wilbur; Harcourt Brace Javanovich, New York; 1988. See "Shame," and "A Summer Morning."

*Hamilton, An Illustrated History,* by John C. Weaver; James Lorimer & Company, Publishers, Toronto; 1982; p. 16.

Nicholas Terpstra, "Local Politics and Local Planning: A Case Study of

Hamilton Ontario, 1915–1930," *Urban History Review*, vol. xiv/2 (October, 1985); p. 114–128.

*Pen and Pencil Sketches of Wentworth Landmarks*, by Mrs. Dick-Lauder, Mrs. Carr, R.K. Kernighan (The Khan), J.E. Wodell, J.W. Stead, J. McMonies, and others. Illustrations by J.R. Seavey; The Spectator Printing Company, Ltd., Hamilton, 1897. The reporter's descriptions in "A Gruesome Ground" are found in this collection.

*Little Big Man*, by Thomas Berger; The Dial Press, New York; 1964.

Mary E. Rose Holden, "Burlington Bay, Beach and Heights in History;" *Wentworth Historical Society Journal and Transactions*, 1899.

*The Trail of the Black Walnut*, G. Elmore Reaman; McClelland and Stewart, Toronto; 1957. The passages about the Loyalist experience quoted in "Flight and Refuge" are taken from this book.

*The Whole Night, Coming Home*, by Roo Borson; McClelland and Stewart, Toronto; 1984. *The Garden Going On Without Us*, by Lorna Crozier; McClelland and Stewart, Toronto; 1985. The titles of these two volumes of poetry serendipitously joined together to become the title of the two chapters in this book.

# Acknowledgements

Portions of this book appeared in various forms in *The Broadway, The Hamilton Spectator, Compass: A Jesuit Journal, Canadian Geographic, Gaspereau Review*, and *Image: A Journal of Arts and Religion*. One of these various forms was an article entitled, "Where in the World is Burlington Heights?" which appeared in *The Broadway*, and won the 1994 Hamilton and Region Arts Council Award for Non-fiction Article. The first two chapters appeared, in a slightly different form, in the anthology *Great Lakes logia*, Joe Blades, Editor; Broken Jaw Press, Fredericton, NB; 2001. "Giants" was published as a hand-set and printed broadsheet by Will Rueter at Aliquando Press, Dundas, in an edition of 35; 1999. "Blondin on a Tightrope" first appeared in *Scrabbling for Repose*, published by Split Reed Press, Toronto, 1982. The excerpt from *The Sleeping Lord, and other fragments* by David Jones is used with permission of Faber and Faber, London.

WITH SPECIAL THANKS TO

John Mercer, George Mercer, Al Mercer, Margaret Brunton, Margaret (Brunton) Long, Victor Almas, Bernadette Melvin Needham, Marie Melvin Jones, Larry Easterbrook, Gladys Collura, John Collura, Ben

Kerr, Matthew Ambeau, Paul McKeown, Steve Schwedyk, Audell Schimmel—for their stories; Bill Johnston, Jon Zemitis, Monique Roy-Sole, Sister Stephanie Vincec—for editorial encouragement; Brian Henley, Margaret Houghton, Paul Wilson, Beth Robinson, Murray Aikman, Bill Nesbitt, Wende Bartley, Paula Grove, George McKibbon, Sheila Torsney, Tim McCarroll-Butler, Glenn Macdonald, Nicholas Terpstra, Wes Bates, Suzanne de Maio, Gretchen Umholtz, Lud Previc, Dominik Bardos—for help, aware and unaware, along the way; Bernadette Rule, Marilyn Gear Pilling, Linda Frank, John Steffler, Jim Doelman, Travis Kroeker, Deborah Bowen, Peter and Laura Enneson—for reading and commenting; Anna, Sarah and Katie—for being mostly willing walking companions; and, always, Mary.

Text copyright © John Terpstra, 2002
Illustrations copyright © Wesley Bates, 2002
Maps copyright © Glenn Macdonald, 2002

All rights reserved. No part of this publication may be reproduced in any form without the prior written consent of the publisher. Any requests for the photocopying of any part of this book should be directed in writing to the Canadian Copyright Licensing Agency.

Typeset in Amethyst by Andrew Steeves and printed offset at Gaspereau Press by Gary Dunfield and Marilyn MacIntyre. Amethyst is a typeface designed in four weights by Jim Rimmer at the Rimmer Type Foundry, New Westminster, BC.

Gaspereau Press acknowledges the support of the Canada Council for the Arts and the Nova Scotia Department of Tourism and Culture.

1   3   5   4   2

NATIONAL LIBRARY OF CANADA CATALOGUING IN PUBLICATION

Terpstra, John
Falling into place / John Terpstra.

ISBN 1-894031-60-1

1. Iroquois Bar (Ont.)   2. Hamilton (Ont.)   I. Title.
PS8589.E75A16 2002   C814'.54   C2002-904086-8
PR9199.3.T434A16 2002

GASPEREAU PRESS, PRINTERS & PUBLISHERS
ONE CHURCH AVENUE, KENTVILLE, NOVA SCOTIA
CANADA B4N 2M7